LADY GAGA

THE UNAUTHORIZED BIOGRAPHY

Christian Guiltenane is the Acting Editor of *OK!* magazine. A showbiz reporter of many years' standing, he has regularly contributed to national newspapers and magazines, and is the author of a number of books on popular culture, including biographies. He is a lifelong devotee of pop music, and has interviewed many industry greats, including Madonna and his self-confessed idol, Kylie Minogue. He lives in London with his partner, and remains hopelessly but happily lost in pop music.

LADY GAGA

THE UNAUTHORIZED BIOGRAPHY

Christian Guiltenane

Michael O'Mara Books Limited

First published in Great Britain in 2013 by
Michael O'Mara Books Limited
9 Lion Yard
Tremadoc Road
London SW4 7NQ

A CIP catalogue record for this book is available
from the British Library.

Papers used by Michael O'Mara Books Limited are natural,
recyclable products made from wood grown in sustainable forests.
The manufacturing processes conform to the environmental
regulations of the country of origin.

ISBN: 978-1-78243-046-9 in paperback print format
ISBN: 978-1-78243-051-3 in EPub format
ISBN: 978-1-78243-052-0 in Mobipocket format

1 3 5 7 9 10 8 6 4 2

Designed and typeset by www.glensaville.com

Printed and bound by CPI Group (UK) Ltd, Croydon, CR0 4YY

www.mombooks.com

Contents

PART THREE: BORN THIS WAY

Author's acknowledgements

Thanks to everyone who has helped me write this book; to my long-suffering partner Marcos, who as a devoted Gaga fan has helped me invaluably with my research; to my mum Bridget and her husband John who have been there when I needed them; and to everyone who has inspired me along the way. Most of all thanks to Lady Gaga who, without her colourful life, meat dresses and fabulous songs, would have made for a far less interesting story.

CHRISTIAN GERARD GUILTENANE

Prologue

Born This Way Ball, Twickenham, London, September 2012

It's a breezy Sunday evening in September 2012. Daylight has dimmed since 50,000 eager fans stampeded through the stadium gates, and the rain that had threatened to put a damper on the evening's events has long since moved on.

All around me, Monsters of all shapes and sizes lurk in packs, giddily discussing what they are hoping to see. 'I hear Gaga's outdone herself,' a slightly camp and over-excited twenty-something squeals at his gaggle of male pals, all dressed in uniform of tight white Lady Gaga tees and skinny jeans, with a dash of glitter sprinkled around their eyes. 'It's supposed to be much better than the last tour, which I reckon ain't true 'cos that tour was immense.'

As his mates begin to debate the merits of the coming show, with one daring to suggest that it has already been controversially described online as 'boring' and 'artsy-fartsy', I spot a motley crew of fans queuing for the toilets. While the majority are pretty ordinary-looking, dressed as most people are on a Sunday, some have gone to extraordinary lengths and, impressively, have fashioned outfits fit for a lady – a Lady Gaga, that is.

Take, for example, the woman in her thirties sporting the angular prosthetic protrusions on her face, à la cover for the *Born This Way* album. She's standing matter-of-factly with her daughter (who looks no older than twelve), dolled up in a low-budget version of Gaga's origami dress, complete with blonde fringed wig. Or the gaggle of friends further along the line, completely hidden behind PVC and lace masks, swigging their drinks through small mouth holes. They seem to be chatting away like a bunch of old women gossiping over a garden fence.

But while these little (and not so little) Monsters all hail from different walks of life, something changes when the show finally gets under way. No sooner do the opening strains of 'Highway Unicorn' from *Born This Way* (incidentally, not one of the album's finest moments) ring out across the stadium, than all the packs unite in their adoration of Queen Gaga. The cheers and hollers they let out are deafening, as if they are voicing the most primal of screams. The sound levels are such that you can barely hear the thundering music pouring out of the massive speakers. But if I thought that was the peak, it's nothing compared to the volume of sound when Gaga herself emerges onstage. I am then left with permanent tinnitus.

London, March 2013

In spite of the ringing still sounding in my ears, there's no argument in my head that Lady Gaga is a pop sensation. Full stop. Whether you love her, like her or just plain hate her, there is no denying that the twenty-six-year-old New York star has managed to cast a spell across the globe with her own unique brand of Gaga pop.

Her stats are unarguably impressive. She's sold tens of millions of albums and singles across the world, scooped more prestigious awards than you could shake a disco stick at and has broken download records worldwide. And yet she is a star who can divide the masses, a perfect example of a performer whom people either love or hate.

To those who have been swept up by the wonder of Gaga, she is a new millennial pop superstar, of a type that hasn't been seen since the heady days of the 1970s (if you can overlook the likes of Björk, Grace Jones, etc.), producing some of the best and most important pop music around.

To others – those who don't get her – she is merely a revisionist, reinventing, quite blatantly at times, what's gone before for a modern audience who may have missed out the first time.

Whichever side of the fence you are on and if you've bought this book then you're most likely pro-Gaga – she has managed to make the world sit up and take notice. Not necessarily with her music, however.

Although some argue that a majority of her songs are top-notch pop (there really is nothing better than bopping to the dramatic beats of 'Bad Romance' or the ridiculous hi-NRG of 'Judas'), many doubt whether they have actually pushed the music boundaries in any meaningful sense.

In actual fact, it's most likely her avant-garde style that's really set Gaga apart from other female pop artists. Wearing outfits that most of us would consider preposterous, she has become more notorious for what she's seen wearing than for what comes out of her mouth. She says her everyday life is performance art, that when she is seen out and about as Gaga it is merely theatre. But is it just a promotional gimmick to give her the edge over the current crop of female singers? It hasn't gone unnoticed that since Gaga's sensational emergence in 2008, performers like Leona Lewis, Kylie, Katy Perry, and even Madonna, have upped their game in the fashion stakes. Whether her meat dresses and condom frocks are in fact art, or merely garments deliberately designed to cause a reaction, they have become synonymous with the artist that is Gaga.

It's difficult to think of a world before Lady Gaga, but hard as it is to believe, there was such a world, and a darker place it was. It's been just four years since she burst on to our charts with 'Just Dance' and her subsequent album *The Fame*, yet within what felt like a heartbeat, she became so big so rapidly, eclipsing the likes of Madonna and Michael Jackson in a fraction of the time that it took them to rise to the top, that she is now setting the pop agenda. She is more than just a pop star. She has become a global sensation, having topped the charts in almost every country in the world, and caused a sensation wherever she's touched down, a feat that very few living artists can boast.

This book is a celebration of the woman who has changed the lives of her Monsters. She may have emerged out of the blue in 2008, but Gaga isn't a typical noughties overnight sensation. Gaga has had a life. Sure, she may have enjoyed a privileged upbringing, but she's had her ups and downs – she's had sex (a lot), she's done drugs (a fair bit), she has stripped for money, been bullied by her peers, and had her heart stamped all over. Perfect material, you'll agree, for songs written from the heart.

And now, in the spring of 2013, Gaga's army of Monsters have her third proper album, *ARTPOP*, to cherish for ever. It's been almost eighteen months in the making and Gaga has promised that it will be the best album she has produced (although she said the same about *Born This Way* . . .).

Speaking about the album just before its release, she explained that she was hoping to split the music into two volumes, and revealed that her troubles during her Born This Way Ball tour in Indonesia, when her show was cancelled, were a big inspiration. 'I love Indonesian Monsters, they inspired some songs on *ARTPOP*,' she said in a blog with her fans. 'I was really inspired by the conflict we had with Indonesia so I wrote some songs about it but they're more metaphorical and conceptual about bringing people together, both are dance songs, one song is a complextro masterpiece and the other is a hip-hop/j-pop/pop song. And it's not hip-hop in the way you know, it's more underground Chicago gay club trap and it's very different from Azealia Banks's music because she's more 90s house.'

She added: 'All the songs are completely different. I wouldn't call what I do "rap", it's more like hardcore glam, that's what they call it underground, spoken word over techno/hip-hop, and there's techno, yeah. It's NOTHING like *Born This Way*, but it will feel like a "piece".' She has produced the album with iPad, iPhone, mobile and computer-compatible applications that will be completely interactive, with chats, films for every song, extra music content, Gaga-inspired games, fashion updates, magazines.

So, without further ado, slip on *ARTPOP*, and settle down to discover the real Lady Gaga, the admirable young genius behind the masks who has finally laid her demons to rest.

For now, at least . . .

PART ONE:
BABY GAGA

Chapter 1:
A Pop Princess Is Born

Once upon a time, long before Simon Cowell had pound signs glimmering in his eyes and phone voting decided the fate of talented individuals, the world was a place where opportunities had to be worked for. Pop princes and princesses didn't just materialize out of thin air via glossy reality TV shows, they had to graft for their glory and spend time to win over their loyal subjects. And in the spring of 1986, a baby girl was born who would one day become not just a princess of pop, but an undisputed queen of the airwaves . . .

It was the mid eighties, a time when people around the world were finally living the dream. After years of economic depression, spirits were high as President Reagan and Prime Minister Margaret Thatcher enthusiastically encouraged their citizens to embrace materialism and seize the day. This was the era of the 'yuppie' – the brash young upwardly mobile individuals who worked themselves to the bone to make as much money as they could (and make sure that everyone knew about it).

It was an affluent time in which new businesses flourished, groundbreaking technology was being introduced, and status symbols were not so much sought after as considered a necessity.

Gleaming sports cars tore through the streets of cities like New York and London, driven by flashy young bucks with waxed hair, boasting loudly into their hi-tech supersized mobile phones about the big-money deals they'd secured. Women, too, were making a mark in business, power-dressing to success in sharp, brightly coloured fashions complete with boxy shoulder pads that gave them a masculine edge.

In TV-land, viewers were deluged with images of luxury. The conniving Ewings in *Dallas* proved that money could provide both glamour and power, while over in Denver, Colorado, the über-beautiful, super-rich characters in *Dynasty* shimmered across our screens. Each week, shoulder-padded superbitch Alexis Carrington would stride into boardrooms wearing the sleekest of furs and weighed down by sparkling jewels, spitting catty barbs at all who crossed her. Alexis was the moneyed anti-hero we all admired and aspired to be. She was independent, glamorous and totally without morals.

Elsewhere, the music charts were dominated by big-haired rockers like Bon Jovi, bouffant boybanders like Wham! and ambitious New Yorkers like Madonna. Ah, Madonna. A figure who will appear many times throughout the story of Lady Gaga. It's interesting to note that as the Material Girl was fast becoming a global icon, with a handful of hits already under her belt, a certain Stefani Joanne Germanotta was conceived by two upwardly mobile techy types called Joe and Cynthia. This probably meant that for the nine months she was developing in her momma's womb, baby Gaga would no doubt have experienced the muffled strains of hit tunes like 'Into The Groove', 'Like A Virgin' or 'Holiday'. Who knows, perhaps she even sensed through Her Madgesty's music the ambition and dogged determination of the young Madonna, who had worked her butt off for years to become the most talked-about woman on the planet. An admirable quality that Stefani herself would one day hone to perfection.

Born on 28 March 1986, baby Stefani was the icing on the Germanottas' already rather tasty cake. For the past couple of years, Joe and Cynthia had been making their mark in the fast-growing telecommunications industry. In fact, they were becoming so successful that they decided to start their own company, which focused on developing ways of linking up computers so that people could communicate with each other – an early development of the technology that eventually led to the introduction of the World Wide Web.

At home, Joe, a lifelong music fan and frustrated rock star, and Cynthia, who had grown up in the parochial Midwest and studied theatre, embraced their whizz-kid lifestyle and worked hard to achieve success. It paid off: when Stefani was around five, the Germanottas were able to up sticks from Yonkers, New York and move their family – which by now included her sister Natali – across town to the rather more swish Upper West Side of Manhattan. Taking on a $370,000 mortgage, the young family moved into the exquisitely designed Pythian apartment block on West 70th Street, the perfect palace for a potential pop princess.

Built in 1927 and boasting a desirable blue and gold Egyptian façade, the building was once a meeting place for a secret society called the Order of the Knights Pythias. In 1984 it was renovated and converted into eighty-four apartments spread over its eleven floors. Each of the suites retained its ornate features and became much sought after – as they still are today. In fact, these days a two-bedroom apartment boasting two bathrooms sells for around $2 million (£1,260,000), while a one-bedroom flat could set you back $7,000 (£4,400)a month to rent.

This was a fairytale lifestyle that only a handful of people ever get to experience first hand, so the particular pop princess at the heart of our story was hardly a modern-day Cinderella. In fact, she enjoyed something of a regal life, and a very Italian one to boot. Mom would serve up delicious and hearty traditional food like meatballs and spaghetti, while Dad would spin tunes by Andrea Bocelli or classic stars of old like Frank Sinatra as the family sat down to eat. Every once in a while the Germanottas would travel across town to see both sets of Stefani's much-loved grandparents.

Even now Gaga looks back and pays tribute to the family elders who she says helped shape her to become the woman she is today. 'My mother's side and my father's side, they are so strong, they've been through so much and they both came from nothing,' she told the fashion website SHOWstudio.com. 'They are just the strongest, most irreplaceable women, so deeply loved by their husbands as well. To be such a strong woman and to find a man that will love you without making himself feel insecure – impossible. Both my grandmothers and my mother have done that. I suppose the three – the trinity of women in my life – have been the most interesting. I suppose they're also the reason I'm a feminist.'

Another close family member who made a strong impression on the young Stefani was her aunt Joanne – even though they never actually met. Joanne was Joe's sister, an unpublished poet and artist who had tragically died from lupus before Stefani was born. Stefani felt a definite connection with her dead aunt, and whenever she would visit her paternal grandparents' home she would be mesmerized by Joanne's paintings that adorned the walls. 'She died when she was nineteen and [my dad] was sixteen. And when my mother was engaged to marry my father, they were staying in his house, where he grew up, and a light came into the room and touched her stomach and went away,' she told *Vanity Fair* magazine. '[My mother] believes that Joanne came into the room and sort of OK'd her for my dad and that Joanne transferred her spirit into my mom. So, when I was born, it's almost as if I was her unfinished business. She was a poet and a real Renaissance woman, pure of heart – just a beautiful person. She died a virgin. And one of my guides told me he can feel I have two hearts in my chest, and I believe that about myself.' Years later, she surprised her father by publishing one of Joanne's poems in the sleeve notes for *The Fame*, telling her dad that she may have died an unpublished poet but now she no longer was.

Back home, Joe and Cynthia soon began to notice that their daughter had a musical ear. 'I don't know exactly where my affinity for music comes from, but it is the thing that comes easiest to me,' she said in her 2011 MTV documentary, *Lady Gaga: Inside the Outside*. Many nights she'd sit with her father at the record player and sing along to classic tunes from legendary stars like Stevie Wonder, Bruce Springsteen, Billy Joel, The Beatles and The Rolling Stones. Even at a tender age Stefani was entranced by these artists. 'The first CDs my parents bought me were Stevie Wonder's *Signed, Sealed, Delivered* and The Beatles,' she revealed in *Inside the Outside*. 'They got me two CDs and they were given to me with a little boom box for Christmas when I was young. They could have chosen anything – but Stevie Wonder and The Beatles? It's totally their fault. Don't spoon-feed me Stevie Wonder and The Beatles and Bruce Springsteen and Led Zeppelin and Elton John and not expect me to turn out this way!'

Her interest in the piano also started at an early age. At just two, Stefani would prop herself up against the instrument and bang the keys above her head, despite being too short to see what she was doing.

Keen to develop their daughter's love of music, Cynthia decided that it might be a good idea for Stefani to take some piano lessons. She reckoned not only would she enjoy learning an instrument but it would also stand her in good stead for the future by instilling in her a sense of discipline as she mastered it.

But Cynthia was disappointed when Stefani didn't appear all that interested in her lessons. In fact, when her mother sat her at the piano with her teacher, her sullen daughter would stubbornly fold her arms and refuse to take part. However, Cynthia was clever. Instead of scolding her daughter, she would merely tell her that whether she played the piano or not, she would have to sit at the instrument for the full hour. A frustrated Stef would screw up her face and smash her hands down on the keys, making an almighty racket – but eventually Cynthia's cunning tactic worked. Sitting sullenly at the piano for several days eventually led to Stefani caving in and trying it out. And the result – well, let's just say the future path of Lady Gaga was well and truly clear.

Looking back, Gaga has only good memories of her early flirtation with music and is particularly fond of her first teacher. 'This woman was amazing, she was a great friend,' she remembers. 'I didn't know this at the time, but she was a stripper. I remember I used to say to her, "Why do you have such long nails, don't you ever cut them?" And she said, "Some day you will understand why I have long nails." And now I do.' (*Inside the Outside*)

From that moment on, Stefani couldn't get enough of the piano and would spend hours running her fingers across the keys. And thanks to years of listening to music with her father, she discovered that she had the amazing ability to play music by ear.

Such was her talent that, aged four, she wrote her first ever song, called 'Dollar Bills', which she says was inspired by a classic Pink Floyd track. 'I still remember the first song I ever wrote,' she recalled on a now defunct, pre-Lady Gaga website. 'My dad was listening to a song – what I now know was Pink Floyd's "Money" – and understanding only the sounds of the cash register in the intro, I wrote a song called "Dollar Bills" on my Mickey Mouse staff paper!'

As her love of the piano grew she eventually gave in to her mother and began to take her practice seriously, opening up her heart and ears to the classical sounds of Mozart and Bach. Although she may not have appreciated it fully at the time, her early tuition would become useful years down the line. 'Bach and the classical stuff that I played when I was younger – the chord progression is the same as pop music,' Gaga said to Clayton Perry in his conversations with the 2009 Grammy nominees. 'It's ingrained in your sensibility about structure and discipline.'

Although she showed an early flair for the piano, she admitted that her teachers had their work cut out for them. 'When I would play I would be floppy with my hands because I was so theatrical and I'd really get into it and get emotional when I'd play classical pieces,' she recalled on *Inside the Outside*. 'I had a teacher who tied a string to my wrist and made me play Hanon exercises, which are fast scales up and down the piano. Then she would rest the neck of this Pink Panther action figure on the string and I would have to play really evenly so he wouldn't fall off the string. I was really good at piano, so my first instinct was to work so hard at [it]. I might not have been a natural dancer but I am a natural musician.'

Stefani's love of the piano developed further as she got older. Every so often her father would take her to Arthur's Café where they would watch a singer called Frankie do his set, which included Prince's saucy song 'Sexy MotherF★★★er'. Gaga remembers that every time he'd sing it, she'd feel so embarrassed that her father was hearing these naughty words.

But watching Frankie and the many other artists who appeared at the cafés and listening to her father's rock and roll at home began to inspire Stefani to take her music in another direction. 'The only music I knew how to play was classical – Beethoven, Bach, Mozart and Rachmaninoff. That's all I knew. Then my father gave me for Christmas a Bruce Springsteen songbook for the piano. And in it was "Thunder Road", which is my favourite Bruce Springsteen song. He said if you learn how to play this song we will take out a loan to buy a baby grand piano. It was the hardest thing for me. I was used to playing these huge pieces that were fifteen pages long and then [by contrast] there were these Bruce Springsteen songs. I opened up the book and there were all these guitar chords on it. It was so confusing so I just started to read it. And eventually I got it down. I knew what the song sounded like because [my dad] played it every day since I was a kid and he would cry every time. He'd say, "Baby, I just imagine when you're eighteen and you leave me for another man." Bruce represents my youth.' (*Inside the Outside*)

Whether she was performing music or acting or just plain fooling around, Stefani seemed to be a born entertainer, and whenever she found an opportunity she'd put on a show for anyone who cared to watch. When her parents took her out to restaurants, she would quite happily dance around the table using breadsticks as drumsticks. When she was home she'd record herself singing along to her favourite songs by Michael Jackson or Cyndi Lauper, and would sit transfixed by music award shows on TV, emulating the glamorous red carpet stars by wrapping a big Afghan blanket around her as if it were a designer gown. Then, with a bucket of popcorn clutched in her little hands, she'd parade around the house as if she were attending the big event. Even then the fledgling star was showing early signs of the design ingenuity that she would use years later as one of the greatest pop artists in the world.

Needless to say, at an early age fashion became an incredibly important aspect of young Stefani's life. And her influences? Well, aside from the stars she idolized on TV, her biggest inspiration was a lot closer to home – her mother, Cynthia. As her daughter recalled it, Mrs Germanotta's wardrobe was bursting with designer clothes, her outfits designed by the best in the business – Armani, Paloma Picasso, Valentino and Ferragamo. Young Stefani was so in awe of her mother's stunning wardrobe that sometimes she'd simply lie on her bed and watch her getting dressed, describing it as a 'marvelling experience'.

'She always looked more pristine than the other mothers,' Gaga recalled proudly fashion for the Canadian magazine *Flare*. 'I have a lot of her in me. I went through periods where I was sexy, then I was a hippie girl with ripped jeans and then went into a tights-and-leotards phase. Fashion saved my life.'

Stefani's love of dressing up eventually led to her becoming fascinated with theatre and at preschool she begged to take part in one of their productions, successfully landing the part of Big Billy Goat in a first-grade play of *The Billy Goats Gruff*. Not content with being given one of the leading roles – though that certainly wasn't lost on the young girl, who knew even then that she wanted to be a star – she wanted to make sure she totally looked the part and set about creating her horns out of tin foil. Once again, Stefani was demonstrating at her young age an impressively creative mind.

But of course, there was still a long way to go before this young chrysalis became a fully fledged butterfly . . . First of all, like every little girl, she had to go to school. And there she would continue to lay down foundations for her amazing future career.

Chapter 2:
Sacred Heart Attack

Naturally enough for someone who lived in a luxury apartment on the Upper West Side, the young Gaga enjoyed an exclusive education. Stefani attended a girls' private school, Sacred Heart, that looked more like a palace than a place of learning. Set in two elaborately designed mansions on the corner of East 91st and Fifth Avenue, the impressive and highly regarded school, founded in 1881, was like something you'd see in movies. On the outside, the building was adorned with cherubs, while inside were magnificent marble staircases, thick-piled carpets and polished wooden floors. Unsurprisingly, such an education didn't exactly come cheap – the Germanottas had to fork out around $23,000 (£14,500) a year for the privilege. But to the proud parents, the sum was justified as they were assured that their children would come away with an education of merit. No doubt they were also influenced by the school's stellar alumni, which included Gloria Vanderbilt, Caroline Kennedy and socialites Paris and Nicky Hilton.

While the curriculum in the school's early days had focused very much on etiquette, teaching its young ladies social graces and appropriate behaviour, it had, over the years, moved with the times.

So when Stefani entered Sacred Heart, while she could expect to study standard subjects like mathematics, English, history and French, she would also encounter a wider range of topics including economics, computing and sex education.

What excited Stefani most was the improved arts programme at the school, which meant she would be able to continue her piano studies as well developing her vocal and acting skills – three of her greatest passions.

But the Convent of the Sacred Heart was a Catholic school run by nuns, and Stefani would discover that the rules were strict, something that she would find restricting as time went on.

Under the eagle-eyed guidance of headmistress Sister Nancy Salisbury, the school was rather rigid in its outlook, with an emphasis on religion, morality and discipline. Ladylike behaviour wasn't just encouraged, it was expected. Unsurprisingly, then, the nuns were also pretty particular about how the girls wore their uniforms which, in the lower school, were grey tunics under red-and-white-checked pinafores and, for the upper school, knee-length blue skirts in summer and kilts in winter. Underneath, the girls were advised always to wear blue shorts to protect their modesty. The nuns were so anxious about girls cheekily trying to raise the hem length of their skirts that some would carry a measuring stick to make sure they adhered to the rules.

While she was a pretty obedient student, Gaga has claimed that occasionally she was one of the rebellious few who did indeed dare to raise the skirt length. However, her best pal at the time, Christina Civetta, now a writer and fashion designer, remembers Stefani a little differently. '[She] was a straight-A student who wore her skirt to the knee, as we were supposed to, and knee-high socks. Stefani was a good girl, really sweet and normal.'

Despite this slight difference in recollection, Gaga is certainly not too cool to admit that while she was at Sacred Heart she happily toed the line and threw herself into her studies. 'I went to a lovely school and I got an incredible education,' she told the *Guardian* years later. 'And I actually think my education is what really sets me apart, 'cos I am very smart. I don't know that my schooling was conducive to wild ideas and creativity but it gave me discipline and drive. They taught me how to think – I really know how to think.'

However, even though she pretty much stuck to the rules, there were times when she still managed to upset one of the nuns. One afternoon she and her best friend were strolling along the corridors of Sacred Heart when one of the teachers stopped them to scrutinize their tops, which were identical. Because Stefani's chest was a little more developed than her friend's, the teacher shook her head, told her the way she was wearing her top was inappropriate and punished her. Gaga remembers that she was furious that she had been singled out when they were both wearing their proper uniform. 'I was so angry,' she told *Elle*. 'Why didn't she get in trouble but I did? Because I walk around with my shoulders back and head held high? If I were to slouch, would that be more appropriate?'

Stefani's early love of dressing up meant that she felt she never really fitted into the school milieu, describing herself, in a passage widely repeated online, as 'the arty girl, the theatre chick who dressed differently and came from a different social background,' adding that although she achieved good grades, from time to time she dressed a little bit too sexily for the nuns. As a result, she says she felt like she was some kind of 'freak' as she strolled along the corridors of the school past the other Stepford schoolgirls.

'Some girls were mean,' Gaga recalled. 'They made fun of me because I dressed differently.' She added that she would wear her hair big, colour her lips a bright red and sport 'crazy socks and shoes' and 'hooker boots'. She told the *London Paper*: 'I was a wild one. I used to get in trouble for wearing raunchy clothes with my uniform. My father thought I had a screw loose in my brain.' As a result of her supposed 'freaky' look, the girls turned on her. 'They'd be like, "What are you, a dyke? It's only women here, why are you so dressed up?"'

But can we believe Lady Gaga's dramatic take on her history? In her yearbook pictures, the teenage Stefani looks like any average young schoolgirl. Homely, in fact, and most definitely the kind of girl a good Catholic boy would take home to his mother. She was certainly a far cry from the rebellious types who hang around in the darker recesses of many a school building, wearing a little too much make-up, puffing away on secret cigarettes and sporting rings in their noses. In spite of considering herself a freak, Stefani was pretty popular – 'because I'm a nice girl and fun to party with' – and won over a loyal circle of friends, whom she is said to be still close to today.

But even those who weren't part of her inner circle were able to recognize that Stefani was someone who was far from ordinary, especially when it came to her vocal abilities. During the school's weekly Friday mass or at prize-day ceremonies, her classmates were always able to make out Stefani's powerful voice in a group, and she revelled in the ensuing compliments. Gradually her ambitions focused into the single-minded pursuit of making a career in music and forming a band.

Sacred Heart encouraged this focus. Every so often the nuns would take the girls away to monasteries for spiritual retreats. While these were primarily religious in emphasis, the pep talks weren't just about spirituality. The nuns were keen to encourage the girls to think freely and to follow their dreams. 'They encouraged you to try anything you wanted,' Christina said. 'When you entered the school they gave us a ring with a heart that you wore facing inwards. To graduate, you had to write a thesis on the Arts and another on Christianity. When you graduated, you turned the ring around, showing you would take everything you had learned into the world.'

At this early stage of her life, Stefani knew in her heart that making music was what she wanted to do and she was willing to try anything she could to get her first step on the ladder to success.

Little did she know, however, that the person who would start her on this path was waiting around the corner, behind stacks of kooky garments . . .

Chapter 3:
I'm A Freak, Baby

One day in 1999, the young Stefani was mooching around a sassy boutique in downtown New York, minding her own business and checking out the coolest clothes. Lost in her thoughts, the thirteen-year-old started singing The Backstreet Boys' 'I Want It That Way' to herself. Now, while this might irritate some people, one person in the shop was immediately hooked. As her voice carried across the room, Evan, the store's owner, stopped what he was doing and looked around to see who was singing so beautifully. When he saw Stefani in her school uniform, he was surprised. 'Are you a singer?' he asked earnestly, to which the shy teenager merely laughed and said no.

Evan then told her that his uncle was a voice coach called Don Lawrence. And he wasn't just any old singing teacher: he was a very well-established and well-connected vocal coach who had worked with some of the greats in music, such as Bono from U2, Mick Jagger, Annie Lennox, En Vogue and Christina Aguilera. Of course the more names he reeled off the more excited the young Stefani became, and she soon dashed home to tell her parents all about Evan.

Obviously Don's celebrated expertise didn't come cheap but her parents were only too pleased for her to work with such a renowned singing coach. After all, with his roster of clients, he not only had the technical knowledge but also priceless connections within the music industry.

When the Germanotta family met up with Don, they clicked from the start. Stefani and her parents were immediately impressed with his credentials and he too appeared to be taken aback by the thirteen-year-old's amazingly accomplished vocals. Despite her youth and frizzy dark hair, Don could sense that this youngster had what it took to go far. The quality of her voice was of a standard beyond her years and he knew that with a little bit of help and coaching she could develop it into a powerful instrument. 'He was my mentor. He is still my mentor,' Gaga told *Billboard* years later. 'He encouraged me to start writing music. Around thirteen I started writing stuff on the piano in my house, so I moved from classical to pop and I noticed that the Bach chords are the same as Mariah Carey's.' In fact years down the line, when Gaga released her first album, *The Fame*, she made sure that she paid tribute to the man – other than her father – who first believed in her, writing in the sleeve notes: 'You are the greatest and most gifted teacher I ever had. Thank you for my voice, my work ethic and my discipline.'

It was around this time that she wrote her first proper song, a dramatic power ballad called 'To Love Again'. It was a love song, influenced by the likes of Carole King and Patti Smith, which she now laughs at, looking back. After all, at thirteen, what the hell did she know about love?

Under Don's tutelage, Stefani was encouraged to experiment with songwriting and vocal techniques, and told that she should try to sing whenever she was given the opportunity. At Sacred Heart, she stumbled across a sign on a notice board advertising a new school singing group called The Madrigals. Rehearsals would take place at the ungodly hour of 7.30 a.m., which meant that only girls with a deep passion for music would be able to crawl out of bed and drag themselves across town to school in time. Of course, Stefani was one of those girls.

When she wasn't busy studying, achieving A-grades and singing everywhere she could, she would audition for school plays. Over the years she landed several roles in productions that were put on by Regis High School, a nearby Catholic boys' school that required girls for their plays. Despite not being very used to boys at this stage in her life, she quite happily threw herself into these roles, playing Alice More in *A Man for All Seasons*, Philia in *A Funny Thing Happened on the Way to the Forum* and many more.

But it was landing the role of Adelaide in a production of *Guys and Dolls* that made her happiest. 'I don't remember ever even thinking to myself my fantasy was the stage — it just was,' she told *Inside the Outside*. 'I was so inspired by musical theatre like *Guys and Dolls*. But it was hard for me. I had a powerful voice but I would never get cast in those roles because I was a brunette. So eventually I bought a wig. At the audition I knew I had the best voice — it was just about the look. So I got that wig and just went for it. I figured it out. And I watched the movie over and over again and read the script over and over. At the audition I didn't even use the call sheet. When I got it, it was the greatest moment of high school. I still dream about it. I still have these crazy dreams that I get cast for that role.'

Stefani's talent was so captivating that people were starting to take notice. Charlene Gianetti, whose daughter was one of Stefani's schoolmates, remembers her standing out from the other girls. 'Everyone knew that Stefani was destined to be a star,' she wrote in a blog on womanaroundtown.com. 'Her talent was so astounding, it literally took your breath away. When she was a senior, she appeared as Adelaide in a production of *Guys and Dolls* staged at Regis High School . . . They were fortunate to have enlisted Stefani. Now, the Regis boys are very smart (a rigorous exam and selection process is necessary for admission) and talented. But whenever Stefani was onstage, she stole the show. Many of us thought she would head to Broadway.'

But Stefani wasn't satisfied with just playing in an ensemble. She wanted to shine. As early as thirteen she begged her mom and dad to help her land guest spots at bars around the city, in cool hangouts like the Bitter End, graffiti-covered, stinky dives that were not exactly suitable for teenagers, let alone good Catholic ones. 'They were jazz bars, not sex clubs,' Gaga maintained to *USA Today*. 'They would have open-mic nights so my mother would take me along and say, "My daughter's very young, but she's very talented. I'll sit here while she plays."' It wasn't just Cynthia who was happy to schlep across the Lower East Side to fulfil Stefani's dreams of stardom – her protective father Joe was too, lugging around her equipment and making sure she stayed safe amongst the rowdy clientele. Stefani appreciated their efforts. 'My parents were very supportive of anything creative I did, whether it was playing piano or being in plays or taking method-acting classes,' she said. 'They liked that I was a motivated young person.'

The music she was producing at this time was very unlike the kind of pure pop that Lady Gaga is known for now. Instead, her songs were more folk-tinged, with Stefani alone at the piano. And despite her age, she put on amazing vocal performances every time.

As she grew older, so her taste in music developed. Surprisingly perhaps, she was never a huge fan of Madonna, who by the late nineties was less a teen idol, more a *grande dame*. Instead she was a big fan of New Kids on the Block and even had a T-shirt sporting an 'I love Donnie' slogan. She also loved Britney Spears, who had burst on to the scene in 1999 with her smash hit 'Baby One More Time'. Although she'd started out as a squeaky clean, butter-wouldn't-melt kind of pop princess, there was something about Britney that appealed to young Stefani. She may have worn a school uniform in her first video, but there was something far from innocent on display. Stefani became even more entranced when Britney started to rebel and grow into a woman, culminating in the sweaty video for 'I'm A Slave 4 U', in which she gyrates suggestively in a cut-off top.

Stefani was such a fan of the young star that she and her friends would scrawl Britney's name across their faces and take the subway across the city just to catch a glimpse of her when she appeared on MTV's flagship show of the time, *TRL*. 'I used to scream for her in Times Square and now I work for her,' she told *Now* magazine years later, after she'd begun writing songs for Britney. 'When I was thirteen she was the most provocative performer of my time. I love her so much!' She also said she 'admired the level of superfan that Britney had created . . . I liked to watch the hyperventilating.'

At the same time, she began to open her ears to newer sounds, branching away from pure pop stars like Britney and NKOTB and falling in love with more obscure artists like Grace Jones, whose eccentric fashion style was no doubt an influence on the later Gaga. At home she would play the Amazonian singer's funk songs 'Slave To The Rhythm' and 'Corporate Cannibal', then mix it up by dancing to Madonna tracks from her *Immaculate Collection* album. Stefani also embraced the music of the seventies and eighties, especially theatrical performers like David Bowie and Queen. As she had a passion for music and drama, she recognized kindred spirits in Bowie and Queen's frontman Freddie Mercury, both of whom not only captivated their audiences with their music but also with their striking looks and stage performances. Once you'd seen an androgynous David Bowie with a shock of red hair and a zigzag across his face, or a flamboyant Freddie Mercury camping it up onstage wearing a crown and regal robes over the top of a tight white vest and even tighter white jeans, it was hard to shake off their images. And it was this blend of musicality and theatricality that turned the young Stefani on.

With her mind expanding and her confidence building, her style began to evolve too, in a way that would astonish the strait-laced nuns at Sacred Heart. 'When I was fifteen I would wear stonewashed jeans with tight-midriff tank tops,' she told *Maxim* magazine. 'I had huge boobs, because I was twenty pounds heavier then. Big frizzy brown hair. Hot pink lipstick.'

It was around this time that she felt more of an outsider at school than ever. Some of her schoolmates thought she was an attention-seeker due to the way she behaved and dressed. Looking back she recognizes that perhaps some of her behaviour was merely asking for trouble. 'For a little while I thought the girls were jealous, which is why they were mean to me,' she told *Entertainment Weekly*. 'Maybe they were jealous of my fearlessness,' she continued, no doubt enraging those who disliked her at the time even more. 'But I think I genuinely used to rub people up the wrong way. I'd talk about things and do things that were ostentatious and over the top and very vain . . . When you're twelve years old and making clothes with plastic flowers attached to them and trying to choreograph your own shows at your school that are entirely too sexy you start to be like, "OK, this is my aesthetic." My aesthetic is in so many ways exactly the same as when I was younger. I'm just smarter.'

Times did get hard for Stefani and eventually she fell victim to a nasty prank. 'I am the perpetual underdog,' she said on *Inside the Outside*. 'When I was in high school, I remember some of the girls from class were hanging out with some boys at a pizzeria. The boys picked me up and threw me in the trash can. On the street, on the corner of my block while all the other girls were leaving and could see me in the trash. Everyone was laughing. Even I was laughing – that nervous giggle. But I remember holding back the tears. My lip was quivering and I was saying [to myself], "Don't let them see you." I remember one girl said, "Are you going to cry"? and I just felt pathetic. I didn't tell anyone. I didn't tell my parents because it was too embarrassing. It never sunk in until later how bullying affected me.'

Meanwhile Joe and Cynthia were trying their damnedest to get their daughter the break she needed to make it big, and were calling upon any contacts they had to help young Stefani get an audition. Sadly none of them came to anything. But by the time she was sixteen, Stefani's luck started to change when she almost landed a place in a Disney girl band called No Secrets. Featuring five supercute mid-teen girls – Angel Faith, Carly Lewis, Erin Tanner, Jessica Fried and Jade Ryusaki – the sugary group kicked off their career singing backing vocals on Aaron Carter's single 'Oh Aaron' and even starred in the video, before launching their career properly with a helium-vocalled cover of Kim Wilde's 'Kids In America' in 2002.

Later in the year the girls released their self-titled debut album, which featured even more sickly-sweet 'smiley-pop' tunes. Sadly for them, success was elusive and the album peaked at a lowly number 136 on the *Billboard* chart. Eventually a frustrated Angel decided she wasn't able to maintain that dazzling white smile any more and dumped the girls to pursue a solo career that would prove equally unsuccessful. With Angel gone, there was a vacancy for a fresh new member. Enter a certain Stefani Germanotta.

Thanks to her vocal coach Don Lawrence's network of pals, Stefani signed up to audition for the group. She was very excited about the prospect. Sure, the music was cheesy, but she was canny enough to know that this could be her big break. Getting a place in the band would give her a foothold in the industry and would open more and more doors for her. Even if she didn't stay in the band for long, she could have got some exposure, be seen by the right people, win over some fans and then do an Angel and quit to be a solo artist – albeit ideally a more successful one.

Stefani was even more excited about the prospect when she discovered that the lawyer and artist manager who was holding the audition for the group, Steven Beer, had form, having already had a hand in the successes of Britney Spears, Justin Timberlake, Aaron

Carter and numerous other mainstream music artists. For her to be trying out for a man who had links to some of her favourite pop artists was mind-blowing to Stefani. She knew that this could be the start of something big.

Despite the fact that a lot was riding on this meeting, Stefani strolled into the studio confidently and gave an audition that left Steve pretty much open-mouthed. In fact he was so impressed with her vocal performance and her cutesy teen look that he gave her the job on the spot. 'I instantly knew from her audition that she had the talent and drive required to someday be a force in the business,' he said in an interview with *Washington*, the magazine of Washington University at St Louis (Missouri). But sadly for Stefani – and probably better in the long run for her Monsters-in-waiting – her career in a girl band barely got off the ground. In fact, she never even made it into the studio. Soon after signing her, Steven Beer decided that artist management just wasn't for him, as it meant long periods of travelling which took him away from his family. 'I didn't feel like management was something I could do well on a full-time basis,' he recalled. 'So I told Stefani and her dad – she wasn't Gaga then – that I wouldn't be able to continue to develop her.'

The news was, of course, devastating, and for that moment Stefani felt as though the world was falling down around her. But then her common sense kicked in; she was young – just sixteen – and she knew that there would be other occasions to shine. History, of course, would prove her right . . .

Chapter 4:
Tough Choices

School and education are boring at the best of times for most young people, but when you're a frustrated rock star, desperate to get out there and strut your stuff, they are even more bothersome. So imagine how Stefani must have felt as she graduated from Sacred Heart, having achieved top grades, and contemplated her next move.

At first, she considered trying out for Juilliard, a prestigious dance and drama school in New York. This was an institution with a great reputation that had been attended by some of Hollywood's leading stars, such as comedian Robin Williams and actors Val Kilmer and Kevin Spacey. Stefani knew from the outset that this school was pretty cool but something was putting her off, though she couldn't quite work out what. So to test the waters, she decided to sign up for a weekend pre-college programme for young musicians, a highly competitive course. But when it came to the day of auditioning, she suffered an uncharacteristic attack of nerves and, sensing that Juilliard really wasn't for her, decided to look elsewhere instead.

Next on her list was New York University's Collaborative Arts Project 21, a faculty of the Tisch School of the Arts, housed at the Conservatory building on 18th Street. It was actually her mother

Cynthia who suggested the course, which would focus on drama and performance, as she had seen how intensely Stefani acted in her school plays.

What made Tisch all the more exciting was the star-studded roll call of alumni, which included Anne Hathaway, Angelina Jolie, Selma Blair, Woody Allen, Martin Scorsese and Whoopi Goldberg. In addition, many of the students who had taken the CAP21 course, which had been established in 1993 in response to the need for in-depth actor training for the musical theatre, had gone on to star in various Broadway musicals like *Wicked* and *Cabaret*.

Again this wasn't an easy school to get into, and only the brightest and most creative individuals would be given the opportunity to attend. But her audition went so well that, at just seventeen, she became one of only twenty students to gain early admission.

At Tisch, Stefani threw herself into her studies, devouring her music, theatre and art history classes. The courses opened her up to things she had never experienced before. It was in her art history class that she discovered her passion for Andy Warhol, a man who would later serve as a great influence when she transformed into Gaga. Of course, she had already heard of Warhol – who hadn't? – but it was here at Tisch that she developed an in-depth knowledge of his work and first became intrigued by stories of his studio, The Factory, a place where intellectuals, writers, drag queens, models, artists and other creative types used to come together to gather and share ideas.

The work at Tisch was tough, but Stefani was the kind of girl who loved to learn. When she wasn't singing, acting and studying, she would be found in the design studio learning how to create sets for productions, which would one day come in handy when she set about dreaming up the lavish productions for her phenomenal global tours. She was also taught about creative direction, which gave her great insight into other aspects of putting on a successful production, from the look of the costumes to the stage visuals.

All of this knowledge was of course being logged in her mind for the future.

And in spite of the workload, Stefani recognized that the tuition she was receiving was priceless. 'I would dance for five hours every morning, then [take] an acting class, then study at night so I could take an art literature and modern art [class], all the kinds of nerdy stuff that I am into,' she recalled to *Elle* magazine. 'Now when I'm being bossy on my videos I know all the jargon and the terms to use [so] that I sound like a smart girl instead of a twit.'

Attending such a prestigious school meant that TV and movie professionals would visit from time to time looking for people to be extras on shows, and it was around this time that Stefani got her break (of sorts) when she appeared on a hidden-camera show for MTV called *Boiling Point*. The set-up saw Stefani ordering a salad at a café in New York. During the meal she receives a phone call and is asked by the manager to take it away from the table. When she returns to her table she discovers that the waitress has taken her plate back to the kitchen. When she asks for her lunch back, the waitress returns the plate with a used napkin tossed on the top. The point of the segment is to try to get Stefani to lose her temper within fourteen minutes. If she remains calm the producers will hand over a crisp $100 bill, but if she lets rip, she gets nothing, not even her lunch. Unfortunately, Stefani couldn't keep her cool and gave the waitress what for, ultimately losing the challenge.

Despite her heavy workload, Stefani's need to perform was so strong that she continued to turn up at open-mic nights at various clubs around the city. One of her favourite hotspots was the Bitter End in Greenwich Village, one of the places she had performed at years before when she was at Sacred Heart, chaperoned by her mother. She knew that the club had a great musical history and that she was playing on the very same stage as such legends as Bob Dylan, Joni Mitchell and Stevie Wonder. Every time she stepped up to perform she'd look out at the crowd – which from time to time would have a record-industry type looking on – and would fast-forward to the day when she'd be able to look back over her life and say that when she was a struggling artist she worked the same clubs as the greats.

Some time in 2005, Stefani took part in UltraViolet Live, an annual talent show at NYU's Inter-Residential Hall Council. Dressed in a tight green strapless dress, with her then-dark locks cascading over her shoulder, Stefani presented two numbers: a heartfelt ballad called 'Captivated' and an uptempo tune called 'Electric Kiss', both of which, given a remix tweak or two, could be stand-out tracks on a contemporary Gaga album.

Although Stefani demonstrated some gutsy vocals, the panel was not so impressed. Stefani came third in the competition, beaten by a funk band called Funky Butter and the winners, Tom Costello and Stephan Magloire. It didn't get her down; in fact it just made her even more determined to succeed.

But before she could make her next move toward superstardom, she had to make a drastic decision. Something had been holding her back, she felt. Her course was all well and good, but she was beginning to feel stifled. 'It was like a sausage factory,' she told *Elle* magazine. 'It was making everybody good at lots of things rather than amazing at one thing and sucking at all the others, which is what I am kind of into.' She also explained that she was getting frustrated because people at the school found it hard to categorize her. 'What was happening was I would go to musical auditions and they would say, "You're too pop." Or I would be playing shows and people from record labels would be there because they'd heard about the girl from Rivington Street but they would say, "You're awesome but you're a bit too theatre." So I was like, I'm losing either way here for whatever reason. And I really didn't care because at the end of the day I really believed in what I was doing. So instead of trying to be theatre or trying to be pop, I decided to do something that married the two worlds and something that I really loved.'

Eventually she decided that enough was enough and that Tisch wasn't the place for her to be. 'I loved NYU but I thought I could teach myself art better than the school could,' she told *Elle* magazine. 'I really felt New York was my teacher and that I needed to bite the bullet and go it alone. I wasn't interested in going to frat parties and doing those sorts of collegiate things. I was really interested in the music scene.'

But her decision to quit school wasn't going to be easy. First, she had the small matter of having to tell her proud parents that she was planning to make what some might consider a foolish move. So after just a year at Tisch and having only recently turned eighteen, she told her mom and pop that not only was she quitting school, she was also moving out of their Pythian apartment. 'I'm leaving,' she told them. 'I'm going to get an apartment, work eight jobs and find my own way into the music business.' Worried that her daughter was throwing away her potential career by walking away from a prestigious school, Cynthia started to cry. However, after much discussion, she and Joe eventually decided it was best to support their daughter in whatever plans she had. One, so that they could keep tabs on her, and two, because they really believed in her drive and passion. So Joe told Stefani that they'd help to pay for an apartment for the first three months but told her that if she hadn't achieved anything musically within a year, then she would have to go back to Tisch.

Little did they know then that the next few months would see their good Catholic daughter take a very dark route . . .

Chapter 5:
Dance in the Dark

Looking out of her apartment window on to Stanton Street certainly gave Stefani a different kind of view of New York than the one she'd experienced at her parents' swanky uptown pad. The people here were different. They were cool, walking around in all manner of outfits – tight skinny jeans and leathers, floral dresses, unruly hair. This was the New York Stefani wanted to immerse herself in. It was the part of the city that she knew encouraged freedom of thought, creativity and individuality. Just a random glance at the people milling about on her street would testify to that; one minute you'd see a couple of goths strolling by, followed maybe by a spiky-haired punk rocker with an armful of tats. Then a spotty skater boy might whizz past, narrowly avoiding the weary club kids who would be crawling home after a long night out.

The Lower East Side was the place for misfits, those complicated, creative individuals who felt they didn't belong in the commercial world and found solace among similar types where there was no pressure to conform.

Stefani's apartment was nothing like her parents'. While their plush Pythian home had deep soft carpets and a family portrait in the sitting room, Stef's humble LES abode was pretty sparse, containing just a futon, a mattress, a record player and a fridge. Oh yes, and her keyboard. Picture the scene from the movie *Coyote Ugly* when aspiring singer-songwriter Violet (aka Piper Perabo) moves into her NY apartment and you probably get the idea. In fact, the cheesy chick flick may have given Stefani a few other pointers, for once she moved to the area she followed in Violet's footsteps, making ends meet by go-go dancing at night – a job that didn't necessarily sit well with her parents.

During the day – when she wasn't waitressing at Cornelia Street Café in the heart of Greenwich Village – she continued to write songs and make plans. But changing zip codes made her realize that she needed to up her game if she wanted to make it big. 'There were so many f***ing songwriters,' she told Blogcritics. org. 'Everybody did the same sh*t, super-boring. I wanted to do something that was original and fresh.' So she decided to change her musical style. Out went the syrupy ballads of old, and in came angsty, edgy tunes, which gave her a new lease of life, creatively.

It was at this time – about three months after moving to Stanton Street – that Stefani took drastic action to develop her musical skills.

Taking drugs, she discovered, would give her a creative ability that she couldn't access sober. Locked in her apartment with The Cure playing on her stereo – in particular their song 'Never Enough' – she'd snort 'bags and bags' of cocaine. She reckoned that like the great musicians of the past she needed to have a tortured soul. She needed to know pain and devastation so that she could write from the heart. She told online music site Shockhound.com: 'It was more [about] the romanticism of Andy Warhol and all the artists that I loved. I wanted to be them and I wanted to live their life and I wanted to understand the way that they saw things and how they arrived at their art. And I believed the only way I could do this was to live the lifestyle and so I did.' She went on: 'It wasn't about getting high – it was about being an artist. About waking up in the morning at 10.30 and doing a bunch of lines and writing a bunch of music and staying up for three days on a creative whirlwind and then panic-attacking for a week after.'

Despite the fact that she said she never did it for a high, she did continue to take drugs on a regular basis, though never graduating on to harder varieties. 'I have had some friends that have heroin problems but I have never done it, I have never snorted it, never really looked at it whenever it's been in the room. I'm terrified of heroin,' she told *Vanity Fair*. However, she did admit that her episode with cocaine did get pretty bad as time went on. 'I was so high I couldn't see the roaches beneath my feet,' she recalled. 'I used to do lines on a Bible in my room.'

In fact, she got so carried away with the drugs that even her friends grew concerned and tried their hardest to get her to leave her apartment and hang out with them. 'I didn't think there was anything wrong with me until my friends came over and said, "Are you doing this alone?"' And she'd reply: 'Yes, me and my mirror.'

But Stefani wasn't 'a lazy drug addict', as she described it to *New York* magazine. Even in her hazy funk, she was able to keep her mind set on her mission to become a superstar. 'I would make demo tapes and send them around,' she remembered.

While she thought this daring lifestyle was helping her become an artist of merit, her parents were beside themselves with worry. They had given her everything she had wanted, sent her to the right schools and supported every decision she made. Yet now she seemed to be just throwing her talent away.

And it wasn't just the drugs that upset her family. Her evening job as a go-go dancer wasn't exactly something they wanted to shout about. After all, what father wants to see their daughter gyrating about a stage in next to nothing while men leer at her? Though Gaga has maintained she never stripped totally naked, she has confessed to peeling off as far as bikini bottoms and pasties (i.e. nipple covers). But despite Joe and Cynthia's disapproval, Stefani actively enjoyed what she was doing.

'I have a strong sense of my own sexuality,' she admitted years later in *Fabulous* magazine. 'I love the naked human body and I have huge body confidence. I was working in strip clubs when I was eighteen. Girls from my background weren't meant to turn into someone like me. I come from a wealthy Italian family, went to a good school. You're meant to live with Mom and Dad until they die. I went against all I was brought up to be; I moved out of home, wouldn't take any help from my parents and supported myself with waitressing jobs and stripping. My act was pretty wild. I'd wear black leather and dance to Black Sabbath, Guns N' Roses and Faith No More. Very rock 'n' roll.'

But if her go-go dancing was something of an eye-opener, then her stage act at open mics was fast becoming just as risqué. On one occasion, Stefani was sitting at her keyboard in one of the Village clubs dressed in a tight skirt, low-cut shirt and fishnets, pretty much her standard uniform for shows. She was particularly excited about this gig because she was keen to unveil a bunch of new songs. But no matter how hard she tried to win the crowd over, the noisy rabble carried on chatting and drinking as if she wasn't there. Now this wasn't good enough for Stefani. If she was making the effort to perform and put her heart and soul into entertaining a crowd, she sure as hell expected the crowd to make the effort to listen. So she stood up, stepped way from the keyboard, slid off her shirt and wriggled out of her skirt. Unsurprisingly, the rowdy crowd suddenly quietened down, stunned by what they were seeing. What was this woman doing? Was she a singer? Or a stripper? Or both? Stefani was pleased that her drastic action had worked. 'I felt a spontaneity and nerve in myself that I think had been in a coffin for a very long time,' she said on MTV News. 'At that moment I rose up from the dead.' Seated at the piano in just a bra and panties, Stefani put on the show she wanted the crowd to see. And the crowd responded in just the right way.

Although she probably didn't realize it at the time, this particular moment would serve her well in the future. 'I made a real decision about the kind of pop artist that I wanted to be,' she told the *Independent* years later. 'Because it was a performance art moment there and then . . . Unless you were in the audience at that very spontaneous moment, it doesn't mean a thing. It's like, she took her clothes off, so sex sells, right? But in the context of the moment, of the neighbourhood, in front of that audience, I was doing something radical.'

But while it seemed she was happy to whip off her clothes in front of a bunch of strangers to ensure her art was being appreciated, her parents simply thought their daughter had totally lost it. 'I was performing in a leopard G-string and a black tank top,' Gaga recalled years later in the *Irish Independent*'s 'Lifestyle' section. '[Dad] thought I was crazy. It wasn't "She's inappropriate" or "She's a bad girl" or "She's a slut" – he just thought I was nuts – that I was doing drugs and had lost my mind and had no concept of reality any more. For my father, it was an issue of sanity.'

Eventually, Joe and Cynthia decided the time had come to act. Wisely, Joe took the gentle approach but made sure his message was very clear. In an interview with the now defunct US website ShockHound, Stefani recalled her father telling her one day, 'You're f★★kin' up, kid!' after she had snorted cocaine in her parents' bathroom. 'I looked at him and thought, "How does he know that I am high now?" And he never said a word about drugs, not one word. But he said, "I just got to tell you that anyone you meet while you are like this, and any friend that you make in the future while you are with this thing, you will lose." And we never talked about it again.'

Until she properly pulled herself together, Joe kept his distance from his daughter, which she found hard to deal with as the two of them had always been so close. To this day, she swears that her father is the most important person in her life and that she would never do anything to hurt or disappoint him. 'As successful as people may perceive me to be, if my father called right now and said, "What the hell were you thinking doing this?" and was mad about something, it would break my heart,' she said. 'If somebody walks up to me and says, "You're a nasty bitch and I hate your music and you're talentless," it means nothing to me. Nothing. But if my father says it, it means a lot.' (ShockHound interview)

If her father's unhappiness wasn't enough to give Stefani a nudge to see sense, the time her drug-taking took a darker turn certainly gave her the wake-up call she needed. 'I had a scary experience one night and thought I might die,' she told the *Sunday Times Culture* magazine. 'I woke up, but it helped me become the person I am. I see things in quite a fragmented, psychotic manner, which I think is because of that. But I decided it was more important to become a centred, critical thinker; that was more powerful than the drug itself.'

Looking back, Gaga says she is proud of herself that she was the kind of strong girl who managed to sort out her life all by herself. 'I didn't go to Alcoholics Anonymous or Narcotics Anonymous, I did it myself,' she told *More!* 'I have such a fear of failure; I didn't want anything to make me fail. So I stopped [drugs]. I have the most incredible willpower and I decided that nothing would happen to me if I carried on like that and I wanted something to happen.'

But Gaga maintains to this day that she's not the type to wallow in regret for what she's done and says that that troubled period in her life offered her some important lessons. 'I'm glad I did it all so young because now I'm done with it. At the time it was like self-discovery and a way for me to feel good about myself,' she told the *Guardian*. 'I was just being nostalgic and creative and thought I was [Warhol hanger-on] Edie Sedgwick and making music. I wouldn't encourage anyone to do it, but I do think that when you struggle, that's when your art gets great.'

And she was right – to a degree. If there was one positive to come from this dark time in her life, it was that it spawned the track 'Beautiful, Dirty, Rich', which would appear on *The Fame* and serve as the soundtrack to the *Gossip Girl* trails on ITV2. 'I was doing a lot of drugs when I wrote [the song],' she told *Rolling Stone* magazine. 'It's about how on the Lower East Side, there were a lot of rich kids who did drugs and said they were poor artists,' she continued, seemingly without irony. '"Daddy, I'm so sorry, I'm so, so sorry, yes, we just like to party." I used to hear my friends on the phone with their parents asking for money before they would go buy drugs.'

If the song proves one thing, it was that even though her life was taking a dangerous direction, she was still in pursuit of stardom. She wanted to be famous, to be successful. But performing solo wasn't working for her. She may have rocked the clubs at her keyboard, but no one was noticing her. She needed to try something different. And she'd soon discover that a little bit of help from her friends and a large dash of help from Lady Luck would come in very handy indeed.

Chapter 6:
Stroke of Luck

Despite her dangerous flirtation with drugs, music was still Stefani's number one priority in the world. Whenever she had time, she would demo songs, sometimes using the facilities back at Tisch, so she could send them out to labels and managers in the hope of being spotted. Sadly, the response was lacklustre, to say the least.

To gain more insight into the music industry, she even got herself an interning job with renowned producer Irwin Robinson at Famous Music Publishing. Located in a Midtown office building, it was here that she would cross paths with a singer–songwriter by the name of Wendy Starland, who would in a matter of months change Stefani's life beyond recognition. But for now, her role was to fetch coffees and run errands for Irwin Robinson.

Despite her lowly position she did make an impression. Wendy remembers that Stefani was always complimenting her and had clearly done her research. 'There was a song of mine called "Stolen Love",' she told Maureen Callahan, for the latter's book *Poker Face: The Rise and Rise of Lady Gaga*, 'and she said, "I play it over and over again; it meant a lot to me." Like, "I love your music." She's very smart. She knows about people; she knows how to handle people. She's great at getting her way.'

Meanwhile, by night, Stefani was still plugging away on the live scene. But as much as she enjoyed banging out her tunes on her faithful keyboard to the handful of clubbers who bothered to listen, she began to feel she might gain more attention if she fronted a band. Over the years, as far back as high school, she had been part of several combos. But nothing had ever really worked out and they had all been short-lived.

Before she'd quit Tisch, she had befriended a couple of rockers called Calvin Pia and Eli Silverman who had been impressed by Stefani when they saw her perform at one of the Village clubs. Before long she, Calvin, Eli and their drummer pal Alex Beckman were performing under the name of the Stefani Germanotta Band – or 'SGBand' for short.

'We used to rehearse at this really dingy practice space on the Lower East Side, like, under some grocery store, where you'd have to enter through those metal doors on the sidewalk, and she had this huge keyboard that she'd wheel down the street from her apartment on Rivington and Suffolk,' Calvin Pia told the *Observer* in 2009. 'She was very bubbly, very eccentric, very driven.'

Unlike previous bands, Stefani took this outfit seriously and insisted on their meeting up on a regular basis so they could rehearse thoroughly. In the gloomy rehearsal space, they would run through songs they thought would work at the clubs. Some of these would be written by Stefani herself, while others would be Led Zeppelin, Pink Floyd or Jefferson Airplane covers. With Stefani on lead vocals, the group started gigging around Lower East Side bars such as the Bitter End and the Mercury Lounge, where they seemed to attract a small following. But the music wasn't exactly setting the world on fire. According to a pal of the band, the music was 'female Billy Joel, like piano rock'. Another friend, Kallen, remembered: 'She'd play her piano standing up. The band, to be honest – they weren't great. I always thought she was talented. I'm sure she realized, "I gotta do something unique."'

So she did just that. To give her a stand-out appearance, Stefani dressed a lot more conservatively than her usual provocative style and gave herself a cooler 'indie chick' make-over, topped off with a hairdo inspired by Amy Winehouse, who at the time was just starting out in the UK and had still to make her mark in the US.

The group teamed up with producer Joe Vulpis, who was an old friend of Stefani's dad and had previously worked with Lindsay Lohan, to produce a five-track recording called *Words*, featuring the songs 'No Floods', 'Something Crazy' (aka 'When You're Not Around'), 'Red & Blue', 'Wish You Were Here' and the title track. It was crude, to say the least, little more than a demo, but it most certainly got the message across that Stefani was a stand-out vocalist and there was great potential in her songwriting. Joe Vulpis liked the band. They were still a diamond in the rough, but he could definitely see potential in them. Or in Stefani, at least.

A couple of months after the demo, in March 2006, he offered to release an EP for them. Together with some reworked versions of songs from *Words*, the *Red & Blue* EP also featured a few new tracks, including 'Hollywood' and 'Master Heartbreaker'. Once they had released the CD, interest was aroused and the band took to the road, securing gigs as far afield as LA, Portland and Pittsburgh. At last, Stefani felt she could be going places.

In June 2006, the group was invited to take part in the Songwriters Hall of Fame New Songwriters' Showcase at the Cutting Room in New York. Also on the bill that night was Wendy Starland, whom Stefani had met months before at Famous Music Publishing. But not only was Wendy performing, she was, on behalf of a friend, also searching for a female singer who was twenty-five years old or younger and had the spunk of Julian Casablancas, the lead singer from The Strokes. Record producer and songwriter Rob Fusari had sent her out on the mission, telling her, 'She doesn't have to be drop-dead gorgeous, she doesn't even have to have the best talent . . . The necessary requirement is that you can't take your eyes off her.' (Maureen Callahan, *Poker Face*)

Rob Fusari had been in the industry for years. Like Stefani he studied classical piano as a kid and even got to perform at Carnegie Hall three times in a row. Later he went on to study at William Patterson College in New Jersey where he started his songwriting career. It was there that he met songwriter Irwin Levine, who taught him a lot about the craft. After hooking up with another songwriter, Josh Thompson, he was introduced to the world of R&B and earned an opportunity to write a song for soul legend George Benson. But it was when he met producer Vincent Herbert that his world blew up. Vincent had just discovered a girl band called Destiny's Child and Rob found himself writing for them, penning such hits as 'No, No, No' and 'Bootylicious'.

But back to Gaga. Even before the Songwriters' Showcase, Stefani was busy networking, dashing straight up to Wendy and reminding her that they had worked together. Wendy duly paid attention to her set when it was time for Stefani to sing – and boy, was she blown away. Watching Stefani perform in Lycra prompted a whole mix of emotions for Wendy. The songs were OK, she thought, but needed polishing, and she looked a bit like she was at a jazzercize class and sounded like Fiona Apple. But her performance was breathtaking. Wendy knew that Stefani had that special something that Rob was after. Mission accomplished.

After the show, Wendy didn't waste a minute, grabbing Stefani by the arm, dragging her out into the street and telling her to ditch the band. 'Wendy came up to me and says, "Holy f★★★ing sh★t, you have elephant balls for a chick." She sinks her fingers into my arm and looks me dead in the eye and says, "I'm about to change your life." And she calls up Rob and says, "I've found her."' (Maureen Callahan, *Poker Face*)

This magical moment sounds just like a scene out of a movie – and to some degree it was. But things weren't set to run smoothly.

Wendy was so excited by her find that she didn't care that she was calling up Rob in the wee hours of the morning. She knew that Stefani was the real thing and she had to tell him about her there and then. Rob, on the other hand, wasn't buying it. Already annoyed that he'd been woken, he was persuaded to look Stefani up on her MySpace site. He did, but still he failed to be impressed. To him the songs were a bit 'blah' and her look left a lot to be desired. 'Wendy,' he groaned over the phone, 'this is not going to happen, don't waste my time.' But Wendy wasn't giving in. She told Rob to strip away Stefani's current look, forget about the songs he'd heard online and trust her judgement. She then put Stefani on the phone, who told him all about herself and begged him to attend one of her gigs the following week. Reluctantly, and no doubt desperate to go back to sleep, Rob told Stefani that he would check her out at her gig.

But when he did rock up to watch her performance, Rob again wasn't very keen and left the club straight after the show without even speaking to Stefani. She wasn't happy, knowing that opportunity was slipping through her fingers. Luckily Wendy was on her side, and eventually persuaded Rob to meet Stefani properly.

So a week or so later, Stefani bussed in from New York's Port Authority to Rob's studio in Parsippany, New Jersey, where he had agreed to meet her at a nearby pizzeria. As he pulled up he saw a girl in leggings and a strangely cut-up shirt, and he thought to himself, 'Please don't let this be her!' In his head, he was thinking his star would be like a modern Chrissie Hynde. This girl, he thought, was a mess. 'She looked like something out of *Goodfellas*,' Rob admitted in *Poker Face: The Rise and Rise of Lady Gaga*. 'She was a little overweight and looked like she was ready to make pasta at any minute.' He took her back to his studio and even though he thought her tunes on MySpace sounded like a No Doubt cover band, he asked her to play something. She sat at the keyboard and started to sing 'Hollywood'. A few seconds in and Rob had an epiphany. He realized that Stefani was a lot more talented than he had given her credit for and that she had that special something. He told *Billboard*: 'I tell you, in twenty seconds, I'm like, "Oh, my God. If I can handle my business, this girl is going to change my life." I said, "You've got to come up here next week, and we have to start working." And she did. She took the bus to my studio every day for a year straight, no exaggeration.' Wendy Starland tells another story – that Rob called her afterwards and said 'It's good, but . . .' But whether that was just to save face at this early stage is unclear.

Although Stefani was new to the professional side of the music business she insisted on an 80:20 deal – 80 per cent to her, 20 per cent to Rob. In the end, Stefani's father stepped in and after more negotiations the three of them formed a company together called Team Love Child under the agreement that Stefani would get 40 per cent, her father 40 per cent and Rob 20 per cent of any profits from her music. 'It's not a production deal,' Rob explained to *Billboard*. 'She was never signed to me. It's me, her and her dad in this company. Everyone was on the same plane. And I'm all for that.'

And so the partnership began. The pair of them worked tirelessly in the studio, making what they thought would be a hard-rock album. 'She would go to festivals like Bonnaroo,' Rob recalled. 'We started to make a very heavy rock record. Hard and grungy. But after three or four songs it seemed we were going down the wrong road.'

It was also around this time that Lady Gaga was born. Or her name, at least. As legend has it, Rob would tease Stefani that she was 'so freaking Freddie Mercury' because she was so dramatic and theatrical. One day, he supposedly sent her a text saying she was so 'Radio Gaga'. Somehow, the spellcheck turned 'radio' into 'Lady' and Stefani apparently loved it. Sadly, however, the truth about the origin of the name isn't quite so romantic. In fact, according to Wendy Starland, it was simply dreamt up in a brainstorm meeting between Stefani, Rob and a few others.

Regardless of how the name came about everyone loved it – it had pizzazz, it was showbiz and it was cool. So with a strong new name to go by, and an insatiable hunger for fame, Lady Gaga, along with her mentor Rob – whom she was now tentatively dating – continued to write earnest rock songs such as 'Blueberry Kisses' and 'Brown Eyes'. But something still wasn't quite right for Rob, though he wasn't exactly sure why. It was when he read an article in the *New York Times* about how Nelly Furtado had abandoned her folk-rock sound to make a dance record with Timbaland that it all clicked into place. Under Timbaland's tutelage, Nelly enjoyed a successful run of hit singles such as 'Promiscuous', 'Maneater' and 'Give It To Me'.

In his mind, this was exactly the direction Stefani, or rather Lady Gaga, should take. And he was the right person to do it with her. After all, he had previously produced tracks for Destiny's Child and Will Smith. He told Stefani: "'Take a look at this. I'm really an R&B guy. I never produced a rock record in my life. I don't know, you think maybe we should shift gears?" She kicked and screamed: "No! No! I love what we're doing. We're not changing it." I'm like, "Stef, just try this. Let's at least abandon the live drums and some of the guitars."' (Billboard.com)

The pair took a break from recording and headed down to Chili's, their regular lunch hang-out, where after much persuasion Fusari finally convinced Germanotta to test his idea. By the end of the day, the pair of them had written 'Beautiful, Dirty, Rich', which eventually ended up appearing on *The Fame*.

And it was this moment when things started to change for Stefani. At the time Rob was managed by New Heights Entertainment, who would send out the tracks they had been working on to anyone who was anyone in the business. And it wasn't long before people were sitting up and taking notice. 'Soon everybody wanted to meet her. Everybody,' Rob recalled on Billboard.com. 'Josh Sarubin at Def Jam invited her in. They had an upright piano there, and there's maybe five or six people in the meeting. Karen Kwak, Josh . . . But not [the then-chief executive] L. A. Reid. Stef sits down and starts to play "Wonderful", the first song we wrote together, and I guess they have some system that when somebody's really good, L. A. gets a secret bat signal to come in. So he enters as she's playing and by the end he's enamoured. He looks at her and says, "Before you leave the building, you have to stop down in legal and sign my contract."'

After the meeting, she and Rob looked at each other, confused by what Reid had meant. Did they want to sign her up?

Well, yes, as it happened, as Josh Sarubin, vice-president of A&R at Def Jam, explained to NJ.com: 'There was something unusual about her. She sat down at the piano in a showcase room and the way she played and the lyrics and the way she acted and sang was just so different and in your face, and you couldn't turn away. She was wearing these crazy white thigh-high boots and a black minidress and she had this presence like, "I'm sexy and I don't care what anybody has to say about it."'

But Stefani and Rob didn't jump into the artist-development deal straight away. Instead, they continued to meet other labels to see who was most keen. Some lit their fire, others didn't. But in the end, after many negotiations with other interested parties, they eventually decided that they'd team up with Def Jam. Stefani was overjoyed that she had finally been signed to a label. At last, after all the struggling and schlepping around Lower East Side bars, Lady Gaga was going to go stellar. Or so she thought. But little did she know that a devastating blow was waiting just around the corner.

Chapter 7:
Def Jam Bam!

Flushed with the success of landing a deal with Def Jam, a giddy Gaga was convinced she was on the fast track to superstardom, and that she would soon be gracing the covers of the magazines just like her idols.

With a record bigwig like L. A. Reid behind her – the man with the Midas touch for stars such as Bobby Brown, Whitney Houston and Paula Abdul – what could go wrong?

So Gaga waited to start work on her album, meanwhile continuing to perform in the bars at night. She just loved to perform and had to feed her need to whip an audience into a frenzy. Often, she would call up pretending to be her own agent to get bookings. In most cases it worked and the more she gigged the more buzz built up around her, which she loved. As she famously said years later: 'I played in every club in New York City. I bombed in every club, and then I killed it in every club. I did it the way you are supposed to: you go and you play and pay your dues and work hard.'

And of course, whenever she'd pitch for a club spot or meet anyone who mattered, Gaga was only too happy to tell them that she was a signed artist, who was about to start work on her debut album. Yes, her very own record, with superstar producer L. A. Reid. Life, it appeared, was just peachy.

But little did Gaga know that behind the scenes at Def Jam, the execs who had fallen in love with her months before were now in a quandary. They just didn't know what to do with her. She had a look that wasn't exactly hot and although her voice was good, the songs weren't right. They were a little off-kilter, kind of like the electro-pop sound that was bubbling up in the UK. To the guys at Def Jam, Gaga was a jigsaw piece that just didn't fit the puzzle.

A couple of months after signing, Gaga grew suspicious that something was amiss. She was eager to get into a studio and get some tracks down on her album, but no matter how often she tried to get in touch with L. A. Reid or his colleagues, she'd hear nothing back. 'He took no meetings with me during my stay there,' she told ShockHound.com. 'I used to wait outside the doors of his office for hours just to have a meeting with him. And I'd tell my A&R guy I needed to talk to him. And he never took a meeting with me. Not ever!'

It later emerged that L. A. Reid was handed a demo featuring 'Disco Heaven' and 'Beautiful, Dirty, Rich' and was horrified by what he was hearing. Speaking on the *Ellen DeGeneres Show* in 2012 while promoting *American X Factor*, the well-respected producer explained why he had made such a spectacular U-turn. 'Lady Gaga comes into my office, she sits at the piano. She has white go-go boots up to her thighs . . . and she is unbelievable. She sits there and she plays songs on the piano and sings and she finishes. And I tell her, "You know what, you are going to change music." About two months later I forgot that I said that and I heard her demo tapes . . . and I said, "You know what? This is disgusting" . . . and I dropped her.'

Gaga, it would seem, never knew anything about this. As far as she and Rob were concerned, the label just weren't being very communicative. Even Josh Sarubin, who had long fought Gaga's corner, was surprised to hear she'd been dumped, only finding out she was no longer signed to Def Jam when one of the execs revealed in a meeting which acts on their roster had been dropped that week. Years after Gaga made it big, Josh reminisced on New Jersey's NJ.com: 'She maybe could have stayed with the label a little longer but I didn't want her to be in the situation where people didn't get it. She was too good. It was painful because I absolutely thought she was going to be my next big thing.'

In years to come, L. A. Reid would admit that dumping Gaga was 'the biggest mistake I ever made in my life', though he admitted that 'Gaga is better off where she is. She's hugely successful and the truth is — and it may not be the truth but it makes me feel better to think — that she probably won't have been as successful with me.'

When Gaga finally received the call telling her that she was no longer at Def Jam, she was heartbroken. She couldn't believe that after the euphoria of landing the deal in the first place, it had been so cruelly snatched away from her. And she couldn't understand why because she was so proud of the music she and Rob were creating between them.

'It was really hard [hearing the news],' she told *Heat* magazine. 'I was nineteen. I did feel like I would die if I wasn't going to make music because it was like everything was gone. The worst moment was when the label called me and told me that I had been dropped. I just cried. I lost it. I called my mom and she cried and said to me, "I can't even put into words how much I know you're heartbroken right now." Someone said to me, "You can't take it personally." And I said, "F**ck you, what's not personal about it? It's totally personal.'

Speaking to *Vanity Fair* in 2010 she remembered the news as the most devastating she'd heard. 'I hit rock bottom and it was enough to send a person over the edge. My mother knew the truth about that day and she screamed so loud on the other end of the phone, I'll never forget it. "I'm coming to get you!" And I remember laying on the pullout bed in my parents' house and I said to my mom, "Can we go and see Grandma?" And we didn't even call her; the next morning we were on the plane to West Virginia and showed up at her house and I told my 82-year-old grandma everything. I cried. I told her I thought my life was over and I have no hope. And I've worked so hard and I knew I was good. What would I do now? And she said: "I'm going to let you cry for a few more hours. And then after those few hours are up, you're going to stop crying, you're going to pick yourself up, you're going to go back to New York and you're going to kick some ass!'"

And that's what she did. Back in New York Gaga threw herself back into the club scene and did what she did best. But soon two people would come into her life who would both make a big impression on the young singer.

Chapter 8:
Starlight from Heaven

Picking herself up again, Gaga immersed herself again in the club scene on the Lower East Side, hopping from one club to another, always looking for a good time. Some nights she'd perform her songs to a crowd of semi-interested beer-swillers, while other nights she'd put on a go-go show that left little to the imagination. The club scene in this part of town was just perfect for her, especially at this transitional time. She had never felt so connected with people as she did here. Unlike her days at Sacred Heart, she felt an affinity with the club kids who rocked out to heavy metal, the extravagantly dressed transvestites and the supercool hipsters who glided in and out of the bars like Lower East Side royalty. She felt that these people were lost souls, just like she was, finding their own place in society. And despite still being devastated by the news that she had lost her contract with Def Jam, they gave her a much-needed ego boost. She loved the fact that most of the people at these bars knew who she was. Her reputation preceded her. For now that was enough to keep her happy while she decided on her next move.

Around this time, Gaga started to adapt her look, borrowing from the local metal-glam scene. 'The rock star's girlfriend – that was the real beginning of my fashion,' she later explained (in Helia Phoenix's book *Lady Gaga: Just Dance – The Biography*). 'I wanted to be the girlfriend of the lead singer of the greatest rock 'n' roll band that ever lived. I wanted to be the girl backstage at the Mötley Crüe concert in the feather dress doing Nikki Sixx's eyeliner.'

Her description of the rock star's girlfriend bore many similarities to her own situation. Around the time she had been dumped by Def Jam, the relationship with Rob Fusari had fizzled out, and instead she had started dating a man called Lüc Carl, the manager of trendy Lower East Side bars such as Welcome to the Johnsons and St Jerome's and the drummer in a rock band. He was everything she looked for in a perfect guy; he was tall and lean in a lanky Russell Brand/skinny jeans kind of way, with a shock of unruly hair and that all-important dangerous glint in his eye. And, as bartender and club manager on the Lower East Side, he was seen as something of a God on the scene, which added to his tantalizing allure.

She admitted to the *Guardian* that Lüc was pretty much the 'first love of my life', who used to drive her around in a green Chevrolet El Camino with a black hood. 'I was his Sandy and he was my Danny,' she said, referring to the young lovers in *Grease*. 'He had long jet-black hair and looked like half Neil Young, half Nikki Sixx when they were young, and the way he talked about his car [. . .] I like guys like that, guys that listen to AC/DC and drink beers and buy me drinks just to show me off at the bar by the jukebox with their friends. That's kind of like an old hot groupie chick!'

Her steamy on-off relationship with Lüc was apparently the inspiration for her track 'Boys Boys Boys', which she described as a mating call to a boy she loved. But eventually they broke up, just after she was dropped by her record company. Years after their split, she uncharacteristically opened up about her time with Lüc on *The Graham Norton Show*. 'That relationship really shaped me. I sort of resolved that if you can't have the guy of your dreams, there are other ways to give love.' When asked about his relationship on

Fox & Friends in 2012 while promoting his book, *The Drunk Diet*, Lüc remained gallantly cagey about his famous former flame. 'She's an amazing woman, an amazing person. Sometimes things don't work out the way they should.'

But Lüc wasn't the only special person in her life. Gaga had also formed a bond with a fellow go-go dancer who would become something of an inspiration to her. In fact, without the arrival of Lady Starlight, Gaga might never have flourished to become the woman she is today.

★

Lady Starlight was born Colleen Martin in 1975 and grew up in upstate New York. Something of a wild child, she immersed herself in the alternative-music scene and would go on to earn a philosophy degree at the State University of New York. In 1999 she moved to London where she threw herself into the rock scene and lapped up all the city had to offer. She loved seventies British glam rock and living in the UK gave her the opportunity finally to seek out the history of the music first-hand. 'I'd have stayed [in London] for ever, if I could have got a work visa,' Starlight told the *Daily Mirror*. 'It was where I started collecting vinyl and fell in love with the sounds of the 1970s.'

After a couple of years, she was back in New York and trying to forge a career in the Lower East Side clubs, while studying at the Fashion Institute of Technology. New York, she claimed, was like living in an art piece. 'I came and felt right at home,' she told Clubplanet.com. 'To me it was all about the art and fashion. Every time you leave your house you saw people just walking down the street wearing something really unique or sexy. It was very much like the whole seventies glam look. It reminds me when David Johansen [of The New York Dolls] said that it was happening on the streets. It was like, whoa! That's how I began my performing career by just walking down the street. Then, I started go-go dancing because I was really into the mod scene and the all-night dance parties. I looked exactly like Peggy Moffitt every day. It was all about getting dressed up, going out, and partying every night. Then me and my partner started doing more performance art. We took it to the next level.'

In 2004, calling herself Lady Starlight, a name inspired by a song by The Sweet, she rocked up to the Niagara bar on 112 Avenue A and pleaded with the owner to let her put on a night for her crowd of drag queens, exotic dancers and club kids. The owner gave Starlight a Tuesday night slot, which she called Lady Starlight's English Disco, a homage to Rodney Bingenheimer's English Disco which captivated the Sunset Strip in Los Angeles in the early seventies. Revellers who piled into the venue dressed as though they had just woken up in 1975, and would rock out to the sounds of Iggy Pop, David Bowie, T. Rex and The Sweet.

Starlight's night proved popular with the cool kids of the Lower East Side and it hopped from one venue to another, attracting more and more fans as word of mouth spread. And wherever she went she would keep her eyes peeled for new and up-and-coming young performance artists such as Veronica Vain and Anna Copa Cabanna, whom she would persuade to appear at her weekly shows. In a way, Starlight was forming her own kind of 'studio' like Andy Warhol years before, surrounding herself with a collective of colourful characters. And her club nights weren't just about dancing. They were celebrations of performance art. She was into burlesque so this often included sensual dancing and stripping. As time went on, Starlight's tastes developed and her nights became more preoccupied with the harder rock scene. As a result she ended up hosting a metal theme night called Heavy Metal Soundhouse.

But it was at Gaga's old stomping ground St Jerome's that she and Starlight first met, and boy – how they met. According to legend, Starlight was gyrating onstage and an eager Gaga slunk up to her and slipped a dollar bill into her panties. The rest, as they say, is history.

Their bond was strong from the outset. They had lots in common: they were both from Italian–American families and they both had a love for rock. Of course, they also liked to perform and to shock so it is unsurprising that their creative minds became instantly entwined.

Eleven years separated them, and, eager to learn and open her mind up to new experiences, Gaga looked to Starlight as inspiration. It was Starlight who encouraged Gaga to develop the staging of her performances from run-of-the-mill shows to something more spectacular, as the *Daily Mirror* noted. 'One day, she was like, "It's not really a concert, or a show, it's performance art. What you're doing is not singing, it's art!"'

Starlight says from the moment they met she was totally fascinated by Gaga's energy and creative mind. 'It was a magical connection – we were inseparable from the start,' she enthused in the same article. However, she was also very much aware of her power over her young charge. 'I'm eleven years older than Gaga and I do see myself as her mentor,' she admitted when Gaga started to make it big. 'I'm Angie Bowie to David Bowie. Angie created his look – she's my absolute hero.'

Their bond was indeed very close and they became inseparable, even dressing the same and wearing their hair in similar styles. 'We tried to give our outfits as much visual impact as possible for the least amount of cash,' Starlight told PopEater.com. 'That usually involved going to the fabric store and buying mirrors, sequins and fringe, and then gluing it on to our underwear. It was really more my attitude towards art that was influential to her, rather than any specific look or style. Do it as big as you can, as loud as you can. Whatever it is. The more shocking the better.'

Exactly how close the girls were remains a mystery, though after Gaga became successful, pictures emerged of the pair fondling each other. Whether the snaps were merely a titillating representation of their burlesque act or evidence of something deeper remains unclear, but Gaga has since admitted that she is bisexual. 'I have no question in my mind about being bisexual. I think people are born bisexual and they make subconscious choices based on the pressures of society.'

As a result of this new friendship, Gaga's look would be transformed yet again. Rob Fusari remembers at the time how whenever she'd walk along the most bohemian streets, people would stop and stare at her garb. Nothing was too elaborate or eye-catching for Gaga: leopard-spot leggings, Spandex unitards, foot-high red pumps. Anything went.

The outfits may not exactly have been suitable for street wear but onstage they were certainly eye-catching. When she and Starlight would gyrate along to the rock music they were playing, it was impossible not to look at them. But the girls loved it. 'I was the one who told her to take her trousers off because I rarely wore any myself,' Lady Starlight informed PopEater.com. 'The attitude of that scene was to shock people and make them pay attention. Not just in a sexual way, which often happens. It was more, like, let's freak people out. It was very basic.' She added: 'People would just sit there and stare. Sometimes I would think that they hated us. But they would come up to me after the show and say, "Oh, my God. That was the most amazing thing I've ever seen."'

As their friendship grew, Gaga and Starlight decided to form a duo which they called Lady Gaga and the Starlight Revue. Gaga had the idea that the most outrageous thing they could do on the alternative club scene was to play pop. This would no doubt ruffle a few feathers from those who reckoned pop music was merely disposable trash. But that only spurred the girls on. 'It was the most provocative thing I could do on the underground scene,' she said. 'There's nothing more provocative than taking a genre of music that everyone hates and making it cool.'

By day, the girls would be holed up at Gaga's sparse apartment plotting their next move, working out which tunes they would add to their set and designing outfits for their routines. They would customize their bikinis, adding sparkles here and sequins there to turn the simplest of garments into a stage costume. Imagine a rocked-up version of the outfits you see on *Strictly Come Dancing*, only not quite so polished. 'The outfits were quite often stuck together with glue,' Starlight recalled. 'Sometimes they held up and sometimes they fell apart onstage. We always wanted the flashiest garments and to be as naked as possible.'

And if their garb wasn't outlandish enough their act most certainly was. With Gaga dressed in electric pink fishnets and knee-high boots at the keyboard and Starlight in black tights and red boots spinning tunes on her deck, the pair would perform well-rehearsed go-go dances, using huge disco balls as props. Later they would develop their routine so that it became even more outrageous. Clutching tins of hairspray in their hands, they would set fire to the streams of spray as they aimed them towards the audience. Don't try this at home, kids.

As time went on, word spread that two fiery gals were rocking the Lower East Side and their following grew. Admirers and those of an inquisitive nature would pile into every venue they played at, such as the Mercury Lounge and the Rockwood Music Hall. In July 2007 glam rock band Semi Precious Weapons booked them to open for them at club Rebel. In the hipster world, Starlight and Gaga were hitting it big. However, the girls knew if they wanted global domination, they'd have to take their act further afield.

Chapter 9:
Lollapalooza Lady

Luckily for Gaga and Starlight, their reputation was spreading. As a result of this word of mouth, they were invited to play gigs across the US, and so for the first time Gaga was seen outside her home city. In doing so they attracted some positive reviews from the critics. Erika Hobart was one music journalist who was lucky to see the girls in action at this stage in their career. 'Earlier this year,' she wrote in *Seattle Weekly*, 'a relatively unknown artist named Lady Gaga stormed into Neighbours unannounced, infiltrating the club with a set that sounded like a mash-up of Billy Idol, Madonna and Peaches spun by a DJ. She wore a platinum-blonde wig and a red American Apparel outfit so tight it could trigger a yeast infection. She looked like Ziggy Stardust in hooker heels and electrified the crowd. "Pop music will never be lowbrow – at least not on my stage," Gaga concluded with a smirk.'

As more and more people finally began to take notice of her, Gaga opened her mind to more influences, in particular the retro dance scene that was popular in the gay clubs. 'I was out five times a week,' she told *Rolling Stone* after she'd made it. 'I fell in love with The Cure, The Pet Shop Boys, The Scissor Sisters, I got really fascinated by eighties club culture. It was a natural progression from the glam, David Bowie-esque, singer-songwriter stuff I'd been working on.' The sounds she was immersing herself in at this time would all eventually become part of her own music.

In August 2007, the girls landed the biggest gig of their careers so far – a spot at the Lollapalooza festival, the American equivalent of Glastonbury. The festival was set up in 1991 as part of the farewell tour of rock band Jane's Addiction, to which they invited some of their fellow alternative musicians. The festival took a break in 1997 and was revived in 2003, when it became significantly more mainstream, attracting big-name stars on the alternative, hip-hop, and punk scenes, as well as playing host to comedy gigs and dance performances.

When the girls arrived at Grant Park in Chicago for the weekend event, they were giddy with excitement. With the likes of supercool acts like Daft Punk, Snow Patrol, Kings of Leon, The Cribs and The Yeah Yeah Yeahs, as well as MIA and Electric Six, on the bill, they were aware that this was one gig that could quite easily catapult them into the big time. They knew they had one chance to make an impression that no one would forget.

Strolling around the park before their show, they watched in awe as the bands played to the tens of thousands of fans who had turned out for the event. The weather on the first day had been a scorcher, so most of the revellers were either stripped to the waist or dousing themselves in water just to keep cool. It felt like some kind of fantasy world to the girls, who were used to roughing it on the cold streets of New York.

Aware that this festival was a major event on the music calendar, Gaga and Starlight made sure that when they took to the stage they would make the biggest impact they could. A few days before, the girls had been squatting on the floor of Gaga's apartment piecing together their outfits – in Gaga's case, a disco-ball bra with panties and stockings that boasted a mirror tile trim. But this was a surprise outfit that would be unveiled onstage midway through their set.

When they first stepped up onstage, Gaga looked almost ladylike in a shimmery blue dress and five-inch heels, while Starlight had pulled on an Iron Maiden black vest. The two looked hot in a cool kind of way, but didn't give the audience any indication of what they could expect to hear from them. To hold the crowd's attention, the pair of them stood stock still onstage for a moment, with their arms held up above their heads, dry ice swirling around. The crowd didn't know what to make of them. From a distance, seeing Gaga's tumbling dark locks, some of the festival-goers reckoned they were about to see British soul star Amy Winehouse. But they were about to find out that this was a very different kind of sensation altogether.

As the crowd cheered their theatrical arrival onstage, the girls assumed their positions – Gaga behind her synths, and Starlight at her turntables – and kicked off their set. As soon as the pair got into their stride it was clear to the captivated crowd that these two women were quite unlike anything they had ever seen.

As they rattled through their set, which included songs like 'Blueberry Kisses', 'Disco Heaven', 'Dirty Ice Cream', 'Boys Boys Boys' and 'Beautiful, Dirty, Rich', the pair of them stripped off to reveal their eye-catching bikinis and began to spray fire into the crowd, just as they had done during their club appearances back in New York. To say the audience was dumbstruck by this performance art is an understatement. But it wasn't long before the crowd were whooping and cheering as the two scantily clad women put on a feisty show.

Despite the fact that their act seemed to go down a storm, Lady Gaga later admitted that she wasn't totally happy about it. 'That was not a performance that I choose to remember so fondly,' she told About.com. 'But if anything, what I loved the most about it was that the sea of hippies and so forth that were there were not expecting what they saw. I loved the shock art aspect of it all.'

She added: 'The audience must have thought, "Who is she? Why is she here? And is this even music?" and I loved that! I inspire shock in people and it's fascinating to me. What's so shocking? I just want people to be entertained in a way that they're not used to and know you'll never see the same show twice.'

After they came offstage, the girls threw themselves in to the Lollapalooza party scene, checking out the other bands and enjoying the rest of the festival. However, Gaga's weekend would be tainted by a rather surprising brush with the law. As she was strolling through the park, a cop pulled her to one side and told her that her tiny shorts, bra top and thigh-high boots were too risqué for public consumption. Gaga couldn't believe what she was hearing. She was at a rock festival where everything seemed to go and here was this cop telling her that her skimpy outfit was too revealing. Back on the streets of New York she had never been stopped before for wearing her outrageous garments, so why were they deemed so inappropriate here? As she told *Women's Wear Daily*: 'There's a huge festival with people doing cocaine and marijuana and he's busting me?' She revisited the subject with Erika Hobart of *Seattle Weekly*: 'It's a music festival. Everyone was doing drugs, I think my girlfriend actually had drugs in her pocket. And they arrested me. It was ridiculous.'

No doubt irritated by people confusing her for Amy Winehouse at Lollapalooza, Gaga decided to change her look again when she returned to New York. This time she bleached her hair blonde, so that she resembled a mid-eighties Madonna. 'Amy is badass,' Gaga later explained to the *Sun*, 'But I want to be known for my own look.'

With a new look came a whole new concept. The girls decided to host a burlesque/pop/rock 'n' roll/glam/metal party night called the New York Street Revival and Trash Dance, which would take place at the Slipper Room. Wearing a coned bra and hotpants, with her bleached hair piled upon her head like a huge explosion, Gaga was almost totally unrecognizable from the Stefani Germanotta who had attended Sacred Heart in a prim uniform. When old friend Christina Civetta saw the show there, she couldn't believe the change she saw in her old friend. 'I was so shocked when I first saw her perform as Lady Gaga,' she reminisced to the *Daily Mail*. 'I said, "God, you've changed!" But when we got to talking she hadn't changed at all. She wasn't even drinking – she was still one of the nice girls. I really think her morals are still intact.'

So the transformation was almost complete. Stefanie Germanotta had all but disappeared and in her place was the fiery, wild, attention-seeking Lady Gaga. But there was still some way to go before she would finally blossom into the superstar we know today. And her old pal Rob Fusari would once again come to the rescue to give her the next leg-up.

Chapter 10:
Movers and Shakers

While Gaga and the Starlight Revue continued to gain momentum, her old pal Rob Fusari had been busy beavering away behind the scenes, desperate to move things along still further. Between them, the pair had produced a handful of great songs that were getting noticed on the hipster scene. It was time now for them to break out and be heard by the rest of the world.

Thanks to his previous work with bands like Destiny's Child, Rob had amassed a lot of contacts within the music industry. In particular he knew a record producer called Vincent Herbert, who had worked his magic on some extremely successful pop artists, including Aaliyah, Whitney Houston and Toni Braxton. It was Vincent who had given Rob his all-important break by getting him involved with a girl band called Destiny's Child, who of course went on to become somewhat famous.

Feeling confident about the tracks he and Gaga had produced so far, Rob sent Vincent a CD of songs and waited to hear his response. Fortunately for Rob and Gaga, Vincent's reaction was positive. In fact, he told Rob that he loved the tracks and reckoned that this Gaga woman had something special. But before he committed himself to anything, he insisted on flying to New York and checking her out for himself. He wasn't disappointed. Sitting quietly with Rob at a Lower East Side club, Vincent watched the young star in the making do her stuff with Starlight, grinding across the stage in her flamboyant clothes, singing along to the backing track and being joined onstage by a couple of transvestite backing dancers. The songs were strong, the vocals as beefy as a meat dress and he could tell that even though her performance skills may have been a little rough around the edges, this girl had guts, charisma and a certain *je ne sais quoi*.

After the performance, Vincent eagerly told Gaga that he loved what he had seen. He sensed that she was a woman who had a big talent and a bigger future ahead of her. He was so impressed that he told her he wanted to sign her up to his label, Streamline Records, which was part of the bigger Interscope label. Gaga couldn't believe what she was hearing. This guy had just told her that he wanted to sign her – right there and then. But after her experience with Def Jam, she couldn't help but feel a little cautious. She didn't want to get too excited again in case history repeated itself.

Luckily for Gaga, Vincent truly believed in what she had to offer. 'He saw the artist I could become,' said Gaga, who to this day still credits Herbert as the man who discovered her. 'He really helped develop and hone my skills by talking to me and introducing me to the right people.' (Sleeve notes for *The Fame*) She would later claim that together they 'made pop history'.

Rob Fusari would also introduce Gaga to another key player in her story – RedOne, a Moroccan producer and songwriter who had worked with stars as wide ranging as New Kids on the Block, Robyn and old timers like Lionel Richie. RedOne – real name Nadir Khayat – was the youngest of nine children who at nineteen decided to leave his home country of Morocco to find fortune and success in Sweden, a country he reckoned produced the best pop music in the world.

But success didn't come all that easily to RedOne. In fact, like Gaga herself, he had to work hard for it. 'For me it was struggle, because I had nothing. The only thing I had was the dream and the way my family had brought me up to become who I am, y'know? I was young, I was nineteen. I came to Sweden as I loved a lot of music that was coming from there and I was like, "I'm gonna go and make it there,"' he told Superstarmagazine.com. 'But it was very hard. It wasn't as easy as I thought it was going to be. So I went there and then I had to face reality, face life. I had nowhere to sleep, no work and with the little money that my family helped me with I could survive for a month or so, and that's it.'

Initially, RedOne had fancied himself as guitarist and singer in local rock bands, but eventually decided that a life behind the mixing desk was more suited to him and he began trying his hand at songwriting for other artists instead. 'There was this producer Rami [Yacoub] who later became Max Martin's partner. I met him at a birthday party and we kept in touch,' he explained to Hitquarters.com. 'So when I decided to become a producer, I called him up and played him songs I had been writing and we decided to start writing together. He taught me about programming and how the software works.'

RedOne got his big break by producing songs for Swedish teen act A★Teens, who had conquered the world first with disco covers of ABBA hits before making it big in the States with their own brand of shimmery pop gems. RedOne produced the songs 'To The Music', 'Slam' and 'Singled Out', bringing him his first taste of commercial success. He would also work with pop star Christina Milian on her track 'L.O.V.E.' However, his big breakthrough came in 2005 when he co-produced a track called 'Step Up' for Swedish pop star Darin, a song which won him a Swedish Grammy and Scandinavian Song of the Year.

After he produced a hugely successful song under his own name called 'Bamboo', which became the 2006 football World Cup anthem, he moved to New York with his heart full of dreams and his mind set on conquering the US. But even after all of his success, he still found it a struggle. In fact, he found it so hard to get a foot in the door that eventually he thought about going back home to Sweden. 'I broke down, I lost all my money and thought, this is not working here. And it was my wife who said, "You can always go back to Sweden – it's not the end of the world. But let's give it three more months."' (Interview with HitQuarters.com)

It was sound advice. Within the next month, he was being looked after by New Heights management and landed his first production gig with singer Kat DeLuna, whipping up five songs with her in just five days. He then met singer-producer Akon with whom he formed a close bond, and swiftly started a company called RedOne Konvict, which turned him into one of the A-list producers that everyone wanted to work with.

His management team, who also looked after Rob Fusari and had recently taken on Gaga, got in touch with RedOne and asked him how he felt about working with her on producing some songs, as she was still having trouble finding her own sound. RedOne was immediately concerned. He had worked with new artists before and had had his fingers burned. He wasn't sure if he was ready to go through it again. But his manager was adamant that he meet this girl, as she was 'the most incredible artist' he had met in a long time. Cautiously, RedOne asked, 'Is she signed?' and was told that she was, although she had also recently been dropped by Def Jam. But he just *had* to meet her and at least give her five minutes of his time.

Despite the alarm bells, he headed into the city to meet this supposedly super-talented young artist at the Sony building. Part of him felt like he could be wasting his time, as people were always trying to get him to meet these supposed artists with big futures, who usually turned out to be little more than good singers with no x-factor. But then, who knew? Perhaps this girl would have something different.

As luck would have it, the pair of them hit it off straight away and all doubts RedOne may have had instantly evaporated. Within minutes of chatting, Gaga was enthusiastically bending his ear about her love of rock and pop music and how she envisioned her development as an artist. RedOne was impressed and realized that his associates were right – this was a unique young woman with a genuine creative spark.

The five-minute meeting turned into a day-long session, which resulted in the pair of them cabbing it to RedOne's studio and laying down the track 'Boys Boys Boys', which was Gaga's homage to the Mötley Crüe song 'Girls Girls Girls'. Their musical bond was such that they'd worked out the basics for the track even before the end of the cab ride.

'We just connected,' RedOne told Guitarcenter.com. 'She played me her stuff and that got me inspired. I told her about my vision and what I thought we could do, and she loved it. We wanted to do something that was unique because I thought she was different from everybody else. It was an opportunity to do something very fresh. That day I felt like a new sound that hadn't been done before was born.' Gaga would later tell About.com: 'He taught me how to be a better writer because I started to think about melodies in a different way.'

It was around this time that Gaga got signed up to music publisher Sony/ATV, who recognized that she possessed great songwriting ability. Jody Gerson, now co-president of the company, thought Gaga had the skills to write songs for other stars and started setting her up for work. 'Getting into writing for others happened naturally, because at the time, I didn't have a [songwriting] deal,' she told *Billboard* magazine. 'I had a deal with IDJ [Island Def Jam] that came and went, but that was it. I don't have an ego about other people singing my songs.' At Sony/ATV she teamed up with various producers as she tried to make a name for herself as a songwriter. Jody Gerson says that Gaga was incredibly focused and keen to learn about the publishing business. 'She interned at Famous Music Publishing before any of this,' Gerson later told *Billboard* magazine. 'And even back then, she was famous for showing up for work in her undies.'

Although Gaga was a frustrated artist and wanted to be commanding a stage of her own, she loved the art of songwriting, in particular pop music. 'I think most music is pop music,' she says. 'The mark of a great song is how many genres it can embody. It's about honesty and connection. Look at a song like "I Will Always Love You". Whitney killed it as a pop song, but it works as a country song, a gospel song, everything. If I can play a song acoustic, or just on the piano, and it still works, I know it's good.' (Billboard.com)

In fact, as time went on, she became more passionate in her defence of pop. 'Music has gotten so pretentious that now it's almost rebellious to be a pop artist,' Gaga reasoned. 'A lot of indie rock bands and singer-songwriters have this middle finger up at the pop world and record labels. There's been a lot of damage done over the past thirty years, with artists saying that pop music sucks. It's low-brow, manufactured, fake, plastic. They say we need to go back to "real music" so we've had to listen to some really depressing singer-songwriters and indie rock bands.'

Within weeks of signing her publishing deal she was writing songs for artists such as New Kids on the Block and The Pussycat Dolls. But it was the song she would end up writing for Britney Spears that really excited her.

To look at her at this point, with her scraggy blonde hair, bizarre garb and love of rock, you'd be hard pressed to think that Gaga had ever been a fan of pop princess Britney. But she had been. When she was plain Stefanie Germanotta, she had adored the pure pop sounds of Ms Spears and wouldn't think twice about travelling across the city to scream herself hoarse outside the TV studios where the star was appearing. At the time she was just happy to catch a glimpse of Britney dashing from her limousine into a studio. Never did she think she'd be writing songs for her. But that's exactly what happened. And it was all thanks to pop star and producer Akon.

Chapter 11:
Akon Steps In

The New Jersey-based producer and singer first became aware of Gaga after his business partner RedOne badgered him into checking her out. After hearing some of her tracks, an excited Akon agreed to get her on board to co-write some songs for The Pussycat Dolls. Gaga was ecstatic at the opportunity to write for such established global superstars, but still felt like she was looking into the music world from the outside. 'I was just thinking, "What the hell does this guy see in me?" I'm just like a downtown New York chick, kind of nerdy. I just didn't know that he would think that I would fly. But he did.' (Helia Phoenix, *Lady Gaga: Just Dance*)

But little did she know that Akon was already more impressed with her than she thought. It was when Gaga was demoing some tracks one day and singing a guide vocal that the producer realized that not only did this girl have great songwriting skills, she was a pretty good singer herself to boot. Coupled with her distinctive style, he could see that this was most definitely a pop superstar in the making. 'I knew she was dope at writing, but when I heard her demoing some vocals, I realized she was dope as a vocalist,' Akon told *B96 Morning Show*. 'Then the next day I was like, "What is she gonna wear today?" And every day she was wearing something new, different, colourful and so eighties. It was like, this is just her!' He couldn't help admiring Gaga's individual style and her attempts to surprise people. 'It shows that the artist has already identified who they are, so it makes it easier for you – you don't have to "image" them. They are already exactly what you see.'

He was also impressed by the commitment she put into her work. There were times she would work through the night polishing her songs. But this focus was in fact partly inspired by Akon himself, who had a work ethic that was even more impressive than hers. 'He doesn't sleep,' she told *B96*. 'I've been in the studio with him until five or six in the morning and his manager will walk in and be like, "You've got an 8 a.m. TV performance." He's like, "OK, just another thirty minutes." Then he'll go do it then go back to the studio all day. He doesn't stop. I used to worry about sleeping but now I don't any more.'

Sleep and rest seemed to be something that got in the way of creating, which Gaga simply adored. As she once heard Akon say: 'People forget this is a job. You know how this is so fun, there are so many advantages that come with it that you forget that you're actually working.'

Once confident that Gaga was getting into the swing of things, Akon teamed her up with experienced songwriters like Rodney Jerkins – a former head of A&R at Island Def Jam – to work on tracks for The Pussycat Dolls' next album, *Doll Domination*. The sessions went well and the pair came up with several tracks, but only one, 'Quicksand', sounded right. However, once they recorded the track, they realized that it wasn't quite the right fit for the Pussycats' album. Never one to let a good song go to waste, Gaga told Rodney that she loved it so much she simply had to record it herself.

It was the next day that fairytale dust was sprinkled from above. According to legend, Rodney was in the studio playing back the song he and Gaga had recorded when Larry Rudolph, the then manager of Britney Spears, poked his head around the door. No sooner had he said hello than his ears pricked up when he heard the squelchy beats of the track in the background. He stepped into the room, his face lighting up as the contagious music and lyrics wormed their way into his head. Almost immediately he told Rodney that he wanted the song for Britney, for her next album. Rodney was thrilled by his reaction to the song, but not half as much as a certain Ms Gaga when he told her the news that it looked like her work was going to end up on her one-time idol's album.

But before she could get too excited she would have to wait for the lady herself to give the track the thumbs-up. After some anxious waiting, Gaga and Rodney heard via Larry that Britney definitely did want to include the song on her album *Circus*, though eventually it would only appear on the European version. When she heard the final track with Britney's vocals attached Gaga was stoked: 'There's something quite remarkable about writing a song when you're twenty and hearing a pop superstar singing it.'

Spurred on by landing a song on a global sensation's album, Gaga threw herself into her writing honing her considerable skills. 'A hit record writes itself,' an experienced Gaga told *Billboard* magazine after she had a few of her own. 'If you have to wait, maybe the song isn't there. Once you tap into your soul, the song begins to write itself. I usually write the choruses first – without a good chorus, who gives a f★★★?'

She told *iProng* magazine that when it came to penning tracks for herself, she'd be a little more experimental. 'Sometimes when I do something for myself, I'll just think about something that I could maybe handle that nobody else could. But I pretty much approach them in the same ways. Writing a pop song and a big chorus, it's special for each song. Sometimes I'll tailor-make something for a particular artist and use them as my muse but in terms of melody and stuff, I always come from the same soul place.'

But Gaga also paid tribute to Akon for helping her to master her craft. 'He is a very talented writer to work with,' she told About.com. 'His melodies, they are just insane. It's funny, I think about him a lot when I am doing my melodies because he is so simple. He keeps me on my feet. He's an incredible influence. It's like every time you work with someone that's better than you are, you become greater.'

Fortunately for Gaga, the goodwill was mutual, and as Akon watched her work her magic in the studio, revealing both her vocal skills and her songwriting credentials, he came to the inevitable conclusion that he would have to sign her up to his label, KonLive Distribution, even though her brand of dance pop didn't exactly sit well with his roster of R&B and hip-hop artists. 'She's incredible,' Akon would tell MTV after Gaga hit it big with her *The Fame* album. 'That's my franchise player at the moment.'

This meant that Gaga was now signed to two labels – Akon's and Vince Herbert's Streamline, both of which were owned by Interscope, which was in turn overseen by record company bigwig Jimmy Iovine. This time the boss really understood what she was about and decided to sign her to Interscope too. So in spite of being dumped unceremoniously some months earlier by Def Jam, here she was with three deals. Yet this success had a negative side. Her mentors recommended to her that if she wanted to take her singing career seriously she would need to relocate across the country to Los Angeles, where the label was based.

The shock request turned her world upside-down. New York had been her home for twenty years or so. Her family and friends, all that she held dear, were there and she had experienced some of her best times in the city. How could she turn her back on New York? To her, it was more than just the town she lived in. It was part of her make-up and she wasn't sure if she could leave its dirty streets behind for the wide boulevards of LA. To her, the West Coast city seemed superficial and flashy – how was she going to fit in there? 'What am I supposed to do, canoodle with celebrities at a nightclub, with a lemon drop Midori in my hand? It's not the same as being in a bar that smells of urine with all your really smart New York friends,' she told *New York* magazine

But Gaga's desire to become a pop star was so great that she knew that she had to make the most of the opportunity so that she could finally achieve what she was seeking. She would have to go to LA.

To celebrate her departure, she organized a little soirée on New Year's Eve at a bar on Rivington Street, so she could say goodbye to her pals and, most importantly, the city of New York itself. She knew that this would be a night of high emotions. Sure, music was important to her, but there was no way she could simply forget about the people and places that had made her who she was. Speaking to *Rolling Stone* years later she admitted that her family, her best girlfriend from school and the friends she made downtown were the ones who helped nurture her. 'I said to Lady Starlight, "Without you guys, I wouldn't be where I am today." They gave me a sense of belonging somewhere. It makes me cry just talking about it, because when you feel so much like you don't fit in anywhere, you'd do anything to make a friend. And when I met the right people they really supported me. I'll never forget when she turned to me and she said, "You are a performance artist." I was like, "You think so?" When people believe in you, that's what makes you grow.'

Her New Year's leaving party was such a wild one that at some point during the night, while she was cavorting about on the dancefloor in just her underwear, she managed to lose her keys and her mobile phone. But she didn't care. At that moment she was enjoying the time of her life with her closest friends.

When her taxi arrived, Gaga was somewhat the worse for wear, but before piling in she said emotional farewells to all her friends, telling them she would never forget them. As the taxi pulled away, she tearfully looked back as Lady Starlight and her gang waved her off. Gaga was saying goodbye to an amazing chapter of her life. But in just a few hours she would be embarking on a new adventure, one that would see her life take an extraordinary turn.

PART TWO:
THE FAME

Chapter 12:
Gaga Says Goodbye

Drifting in out of sleep, a woozy Gaga thought about her future. In a matter of hours, she would be on the west side of America, living and working in the city where wannabe glamazons and airhead socialites sipped cocktails and shopped on Rodeo Drive. Life, she realized, was about to become very different.

At last she was about to embark on her musical career for real. No more schlepping around grotty backstreet bars, go-go dancing, or recording songs on a four-track. She was going to be holed up in a classy recording studio, with state-of-the-art recording equipment and top producers, living the life of a pop star.

Of course, her love for her friends back in New York was so strong she couldn't help but feel sad that she was leaving them behind. But she knew that she would never forget Lady Starlight and the gang. Wherever she was in the world, they would always have a place in her heart.

When she landed at LAX, Gaga, wearing her blouse inside-out, was feeling hungover and bleary-eyed. But she only had herself to blame – she had quaffed so much booze the night before at her farewell party that she was lucky she was able to walk.

But ever the trouper, the fragile singer jumped in a cab with all her belongings and headed straight to the world-famous Record Plant studio, knowing that RedOne was ready and waiting for her there.

Pulling up outside the building, Lady Gaga was awestruck. This was a proper studio, not some low-budget backstreet outfit. This was the very studio in which music greats John Lennon, Stevie Wonder, Bruce Springsteen, Madonna, Michael Jackson, Rihanna and Barbra Streisand had recorded their albums. And here she was, about to lay down some tracks of her own in a studio that boasted a legendary history.

'Record Plant is one of the biggest, most amazing studios ever,' Gaga told *Billboard*. 'It was so different for me as someone who was always working out of my apartment or home studios – you walk in and Kanye's mixing his record, Snoop Dogg's down the hall, Teddy Riley's there.'

The studio that RedOne had booked out was unlike anything Gaga had experienced before. The mixing desk was huge, the decoration plush and she couldn't help but feel for the first time like a proper pop star. Not only was she impressed with the layout, she was equally tickled by the fact that runners and interns would frequently pop their heads into the studio to ask if any refreshments were required. Gaga suddenly felt like she was in the big time and for a moment all thoughts of cold, wintry New York disappeared.

Despite all the dazzling technology around them, she and RedOne set about work using their trusted Apple MacBook Pros to programme the beats for the song.

Within minutes, she and RedOne were conjuring up a tune that they reckoned had energy and spunk. As RedOne offered up a few chords, Gaga, still feeling the effects from the previous night's festivities, started ad-libbing over the top: 'I've had a little bit too much . . .' Within ten to twenty minutes the song started to take shape and they had laid down the basics of the track. Gaga's new manager since she'd signed with Interscope, Troy Carter, popped into see how they were going, heard their early efforts and was staggered by what they had achieved in such a short time.

The song 'Just Dance', she would later explain, was a reaction to her leaving her party lifestyle behind back East. 'It's an ode to New York and being out in the clubs, getting too drunk and [knowing] you should really go home, but instead of going home you just dance through it and get yourself through the night,' she told *iProng* magazine. She similarly told *HX* magazine: 'I was taken very quickly out of my party lifestyle. I wrote it instantly – like it flew out of my body. If you've ever been so high that it's, like, scary, the only way you can deal with it is not deal with it, so you just kind of dance through the intoxication . . . Like you do in all stretches of life, when obstacles come, dance through it.'

Gaga was pleased with the reactions to the song. Vincent Herbert gave it the thumbs-up, as did Leah Landon (who had also joined the management team), who told her the song was sensational. Not bad for a track that was written in a matter of minutes. She was surprised how quickly the song had developed, especially when she considered how hard it had been for her back in New York to put together an album she was happy with.

Now, in a new city, surrounded by professionals, she was learning that writing good music was about going with the flow and not trying too hard to push boundaries. 'I was trying to be so cool with my own music but I would get better responses when I would write for other artists because I wasn't trying to be cool,' she told *HX* magazine. 'So when I did "Just Dance" that was my way of being like, "Just f★★★ing write a good song! Stop worrying about what's going to fly in the underground. Worry about writing a great record." It was almost like a switch went off in my brain and I figured out how to write a good pop song.'

When mentor Akon heard the track he freaked out and demanded that he appear on the record along with Colby O'Donis, one of the acts from his other record label, Konvict. 'Lady Gaga is a great person and a cool person to hang out with,' Colby said of the collaboration, adding to Kidzworld.com: 'She's definitely a unique person to work with. I had a lot of fun doing "Just Dance" with her. Her style is amazing, it's great.'

Word spread that Gaga had created an amazing song and around the record label a buzz began to build that a star was on the cusp of success. Martin Kierszenbaum, head of A&R at Interscope and president of its imprint Cherrytree Records, passed a rough mix of 'Just Dance' on to mix engineer Robert Orton, who recalled his reaction to SoundOnSound.com: 'I flipped. You can never tell for sure whether something is going to be successful or not, but the second I heard it, it sounded like a huge hit, it was just amazing. That's how I got involved with that project, and with RedOne, for whom I've since mixed quite a few things. Nobody else was present for the mix, it was just me at Sarm 3 [a mixing studio in London]. I spoke to RedOne on the phone before and during the mix, and to Lady Gaga afterwards, to get a sense of exactly what they wanted, and I made adjustments to the mix from that.'

Over the next few weeks, Gaga and RedOne threw themselves into writing more tracks for what would become *The Fame*, using inspiration from Gaga's life. 'The album,' she would later tell *Elle* magazine, 'is the story of me and my friends and our lives in New York – and you either want to know about it and be part of it or you don't. I am completely 100 per cent honest in what I do and who I am and I've got nothing to hide.' Indeed, she admitted that she wrote only about what she had experienced first-hand, whether it was about sex, pornography, art, drugs or alcohol. 'Why would anyone care to listen to me if I wasn't an expert in what I write about?'

The next song they worked on was 'Poker Face', a tune she hinted was about a lot of things, but seemed to anyone who listened to it pretty preoccupied with bisexuality. She would later explain that the line in the chorus about some guy 'bluffin' with her muffin' was a reference to a girl who during sex with a man was fantasizing about sleeping with a woman.

Her songwriting was flowing and she was producing material that she was immensely happy with in just a short time. She was different to other writers in that when she set about creating a song, she thought about the full production. Not just the sound, but what would happen should the song ever be performed live. 'I always have a vision,' she would later explain to the *Guardian*. 'When I am writing a song I am always thinking about the clothes and the way I'm going to sing. It's not just a song and I'm not just going to stand onstage and sing.'

Working with RedOne was a joy for Gaga. 'He is my heart and soul of my universe,' she said to About.com. 'I met him and he completely 150,000 per cent wrapped his arms around my talent and it was like we needed each other. His influence on me has been tremendous. I really couldn't have done this without him.'

But RedOne wasn't the only one who was contributing to what would become *The Fame*. Of course, she already had in the bank the songs – 'Again Again', 'Disco Heaven', 'Brown Eyes', 'Beautiful, Dirty, Rich' and 'Paparazzi' – that she had written and recorded with her old flame Rob Fusari, but her record company were keen for her to try out other up-and-coming producers who they felt would bring the best out in their new protégée.

Cherrytree Records president Martin Kierszenbaum introduced Gaga to Parisian DJ Nick Dresti, aka Space Cowboy. By this stage he had made a name for himself in clubs across Europe, in particular London, and had already released two albums. However, what had really got him noticed by the folks at Cherrytree Records was his single 'My Egyptian Lover', which had gone down a storm in the UK, thanks to some support from Radio 1. Kierszenbaum was convinced that Space Cowboy and Gaga were a match made in heaven. And he was to be proved right.

'I remember our first conversation was on the phone,' recalls Space Cowboy of the first time he and Lady Gaga spoke. 'She was talking about sequins, disco balls, Prince, David Bowie and body paint. Basically, she was speaking my language.' He added: 'We figured out that we shared pretty much the same experiences, we'd both been doing similar things on opposite sides of the Atlantic.' (ladygaga.wiki.com) The pair finally met in the studio and, together with Flo Rida, penned the track 'Starstruck' and another called 'Christmas Tree', both of which Gaga would later describe as what it would sound like if she and Space Cowboy had babies.

Gaga also wrote a handful of tracks with Martin Kierszenbaum himself, such as the syrupy Eurotrash 'Eh, Eh (Nothing Else I Can Say)', 'I Like It Rough' and 'The Fame'.

Throughout the writing process, Gaga was intent on producing pure pop music with a dance twist. Despite the fact she herself had gone through a period when she felt she had to produce music that pushed the envelope, she also recalled the simple times as a teenager when she would scream herself hoarse as she clamoured to get a look at teen idol stars like Britney or NKOTB. She reckoned it was sad that young superfans rarely had stars to go crazy about any more. 'We've lost that desire to eat the artist and it's something that I want to bring back, but in a cool way,' she claimed in *New York* magazine. But that didn't mean that her songs were going to be fluffy and meaningless. She wanted every song to speak from her heart, and to give listeners an insight into her life. And she wanted to make sure that even though she was presenting herself as a pop artist, she wasn't a pop puppet. Sure, she was blonde, sure, she was often in her underwear, but that didn't mean she was some mindless pop pixie who would sing and dance on cue.

In fact, she was also pretty excited about presenting herself as a strong, opinionated and sexually confident young woman. 'Americans are quite hard on women for sexuality,' she said in an interview for Australian magazine *The Age* after the release of *The*

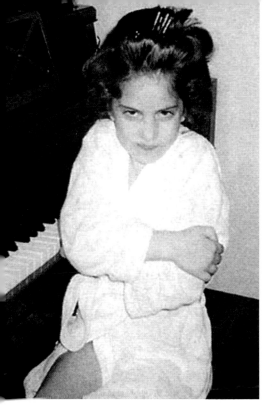

Born this way: a young Stefani Germanotta perched on a piano stool (*top left*). Her expression proves that she did not at first take to piano tuition.

Her adoring parents Joseph (*top right*, pictured dancing with a teenage Gaga) and Cynthia (*left*),who both encouraged their daughter's love of music – despite her initial resistance.

(*right*) Taking shape: Lady Gaga and the Starlight Revue hit the big time when they performed at 2007's Lollapalooza Festival.

(*below*) Lady Gaga and Lady Starlight at New York's Slipper Room in October 2007.

(*top right and far right*) Gaga takes her performance art to a new level by experimenting with an array of outrageous outfits.

(*bottom right*) Quintessentially British: dressed as a teapot to perform at London's 2009 BRIT Awards with Neil Tennant (*left*) and Brandon Flowers.

(*far left*) Lady Gaga has arrived: onstage in California in 2009.

(*top left*) Making a name for herself: drinking from the infamous purple china teacup on *Friday Night With Jonathan Ross*.

(*top right*) Lüc Carl, Lady Gaga's on–off boyfriend – the Danny to her Sandy.

(*bottom*) Kicking up a storm in the muddy fields of Glastonbury, also in 2009.

Making a splash: (*top*) clutching her 2009 MTV Music Video Award for Best New Artist and sporting one of her many outfits of the evening.

(*bottom*) Standing up for gender equality at a march in Washington DC in 2009.

(*top left*) Offstage as well as on, Gaga enjoys experimenting with new looks.

(*bottom left*) Going it alone: The Fame Ball Tour in action in March 2009.

NATIONAL EQUALITY MARCH

A meeting of minds: the reigning Queen of Pop meets
the next in line to the throne at the Marc Jacobs 2010
spring fashion show in New York, September 2009.

Fame. 'But it's really who I am and what I feel comfortable with. If anything,' she continued, clearly overlooking the continuing success of boundary-pushers like Madonna and Rihanna, 'I'm probably the only pop singer on the planet whose record label would prefer if she toned it down.'

She was similarly forward on her song 'LoveGame', in which she asks a fella if he will allow her to ride on his, er, disco stick. Gaga would later explain that the reference was – surprise, surprise – a metaphor for a penis and that she had actually been inspired to write the song after she spotted a sexy guy in a club and asked him that very question. Whether the lucky man obliged and let her jump on top she never revealed, but both the song and a kooky new phrase were born out of that incident.

Eventually, Gaga had amassed enough songs to be considered for an album and she sat down with her label team to work out which tunes would make the cut. Understandably, the job was tough. After all, she had created a whole host of songs that to her ear sounded perfect. But listening to the tunes again, she eventually whittled them down to the ones she felt best reflected her as an artist and as a woman. Once she had made her selection she stepped back and presented the album to her label, who were unanimous in their love for it. Listening to it confirmed their belief that they had a woman in their midst who was not just another pop singer. She was a supremely talented singer-songwriter who was really going places.

Akon would later say of Gaga on MTV News, 'She's brave. She's fresh. She's different. She's bold. She don't give a damn. You gotta take her as she is. That's the beauty of it. You're forced to like her that way she is without no extra stuff added. She's like a sister to me.'

So Gaga and her team were pleased with the record. All that was left was to see how the public would take to her unique brand of dance pop. Would they be swept up in the majesty of her supercool sounds? In April 2008, Gaga would find out . . .

Chapter 13:
Building the Haus of Gaga

Ever since she was at college in New York, Gaga had been obsessed with Andy Warhol and his studio of creatives. She was fascinated by the individuals he had surrounded himself with at The Factory in New York, and admired the way he was able to attract the coolest, artiest people to serve as his muses.

Even during the early days when she was writing songs and performing in dive bars on the Lower East Side, she was thinking about this concept of assembling a group of like-minded people so that when she was ready to step out and be counted, she had the best team around her to help bring her ideas to fruition. Ever since she'd started songwriting she thought about the bigger picture, not just the song itself. 'It's all about everything altogether – performance art, pop performance art, fashion,' she said. 'For me, it's everything coming together and being a real story that will bring back the superfan. I want to bring that back. I want the imagery to be so strong that fans will want to eat and taste and lick every part of us.' (*New Statesman*)

And so when it looked like her music career was about to get off the ground, she began to call upon her creative friends to help her achieve her visual dreams. She later described the Haus as her creative team and explained that it had come about organically. 'I was a bit frustrated at the beginning, being so new to the business and going forward with a major label. I wanted to put my own money into the show because, when you're a new artist, you kind of have to prove yourself. I was making money as a songwriter and I didn't want a condo or a car because I don't drive and I'm never f★★★ing home, so I just wanted to put all my money into my performance. So I called all my coolest art friends and we sat in a room and I said that I wanted to make my face light up. Or that I wanted to make my cane light up. Or that I wanted to make a pair of dope sunglasses. Or that I want to make video glasses, or whatever it was that I wanted to do. It's a whole amazing creative process that's completely separate from the label.' (www.haus-of-gaga.com)

One of the key players in the Haus of Gaga was Matty 'Dada' Williams, whom she had met upon her arrival in LA and briefly dated. 'Dada is quite brilliant and we were crazy lovers,' Gaga told the *Sunday Times*. 'But I stopped it when we discovered what a strong creative connection we had. I didn't want it just to be about careless love.'

Fashion fanatic Matt Williams grew up in Central California, lived in LA for three years and relocated to New York at twenty with the intention of studying fashion at Parsons School of Design. Unfortunately, he didn't get accepted on the course. Not one to let a setback kill off his dreams, he took a sidestep and started working with pattern cutters and machinists, learning the business from a different angle. It wasn't long before he ended up getting the chance to design a line for fashion brand Corpus. After that, his career really took off and he landed a job working for Kanye West's creative team. Working backstage on the rapper's Glow in the Dark Tour, he learnt about stage design and prop building. His crowning glory came when he helped design Kanye's LED light–up jacket that he wore at the MTV Awards in 2007. 'I just found myself learning all these abstract things that you can't really learn unless you're actually in there doing it,' he told *i-D* magazine.

Matt met Gaga for the first time at a sushi restaurant in LA and they immediately hit it off. 'I showed her around the city,' he recalled. 'She said, "Oh, you make clothes, will you make me stuff for my artist showcase?" She liked the idea of something with crystals, so I made her glowing disco stick and we started working together from there.'

As he got to know her better, he realized that this girl was different to all the other wannabe pop stars he'd encountered along the way, even though at this point she still hadn't even finished her album. But just speaking to her, listening to her wacky ideas, he knew that there was more to this woman than met the eye. 'She was really smart,' Matty told *i-D*. 'She wasn't a one-trick pony. She had so many ideas, great style, amazing musical talent, she wrote all her own songs.' When she invited him round to the studio to listen to the tracks she was working on, he admitted that he was 'mesmerized and blown away by her talent'.

Even before she had released her first single, Gaga was busy touring LA's gay clubs, trying to win over fans. To accompany her song 'LoveGame' – the song with the infamous 'disco stick' line – Gaga asked Matty if he was able to produce for her a prop that would whip the crowd into a frenzy. Rising to the challenge, he conjured up a disco stick that would mesmerize the gays when she waved it round. 'A lot of the time she would just get up on the bar and just rock it, just kill it,' he recalled in *i-D* magazine. 'The light on the disco stick in a small dark room was so crazy.' He added, 'I feel so lucky to be working with Lady Gaga, my best friend. We have such an amazing family for a team and just being able to hang out with people I really respect is so great. I'm happy.'

Many of the people who helped Gaga at this time became founder members of her fledgling Haus – Troy Carter, Vincent Herbert,

Space Cowboy. Anyone who inspired or assisted her on her journey was swiftly sworn in. It would be a collective that would grow in size over the subsequent years and bring Gaga's eccentric ideas to life. But first, Gaga had a single to release . . .

★

The Fame album had been a long time in gestation. Now, almost two and a half years since Gaga recorded the earliest of the songs in New York with Rob Fusari, the public was about to hear her efforts. But it was one of the songs that she had written in LA that was chosen as her first single.

'Just Dance', the tune about being drunk that she and RedOne had penned in around twenty minutes the day she arrived hungover from New York, was set to be released on 8 April 2008 in the US. Gaga was proud of the song and believed in its message. 'The catalyst for making music and all art is to make something that's beautiful,' she said. 'I've always believed that art is beauty and beauty is art. I wanted to make a beautiful record. I think "Just Dance" is.' She added: 'Everyone is looking for a song that really speaks to the joy in our souls and in our hearts . . . It's just one of those records. It feels really good and when you listen to it, it makes you feel good inside. It's as simple as that. I don't think it's rocket science when it comes to the heart, I think it's a heart theme song.' (www.artistdirect.com)

To promote the single, Gaga was required to shoot a video, which prompted great excitement. For years she'd watched promo clips on MTV, hoping that one day she would have one of her own. Now she was getting the chance to star in a glamorous, supercool video that would be seen around the world.

As ever, Gaga had bundles of ideas for the video herself. In fact, she already had in her mind exactly how she wanted it to look. So fixed was she on her own treatment that she begged her bosses to let her take the reins and produce the video with the help of close friend and newly appointed creative director Matty Williams. But conscious that Gaga was still something of a novice, they advised that it might be best to leave the hard work of producing the promo to a professional. Enter Melina Matsoukas, an NYU graduate with an impressive CV, having worked with Beyoncé on 'Green Light', on 'Bleeding Love' for Leona Lewis, plus 'Wow' and 'In My Arms' for Kylie Minogue, to name a few. Gaga was impressed by her pedigree and sat down with Melina to run through what she envisaged. Luckily, Melina was up for the same kind of vibe that Gaga was after and the video concept took shape. The eventual premise was the aftermath of a wild house party. Gaga said that the video was a visual of the last twenty-two years of her life, telling MTV News: 'All these ideas and all these things I have cared about forever are now in the room and we're shooting it and putting lipstick on it.'

Although she may not have had complete creative control, the eventual video was pretty much a Haus of Gaga production. The mirror-tiled disco-ball bra top she wore in the video was home-made, just like the ones she wore back in New York with Lady Starlight, and there were cameos aplenty from members of the Haus, including Akon sprawled across a couch, Space Cowboy working the decks and Colby O'Donis popping up midway through to deliver his rap.

Gaga loved being part of the shoot, her first big production. 'It was so fun, it was amazing,' she told About.com. 'For me it was like being on a Martin Scorsese set. I've been so low-budget for so long, and to have this incredibly amazing video was really very humbling.'

However, she went on to explain that even though Melina was overseeing the whole shoot, her own mind was still in overdrive. 'I don't really talk to everybody. I'm not like the party girl running around. I might even seem to be a bit of a diva. I'm sort of with myself, in my work headspace worrying about costumes, and if extras look right, and placement. I don't just show up for things, you know. That video was a vision of mine. It was Melina the director who wanted to do something, to have a performance art aspect that was so pop but it was still commercial, but that felt like lifestyle. It was all those things, I love it.'

She also realized that in Melina she had found a like-minded director who really understood her vision. 'She is a genius,' she gushed to About.com. 'She's from New York and working with her was one of the greatest creative experiences I've had yet. My vision for the video was a house party in Brooklyn but with the sentiment and glamour and filth of a downtown soirée or trashfest, with a touch of my Italian gaud and fascination with mobster movie motifs.'

What Gaga also liked was that Melina was able to deal with her crazy moments, as she confided to an Australian radio show: 'Throughout the entire day, if you could have recorded what Melina was saying to me while I was performing . . . She was like, "No Gaga, stop humping the whale, Gaga, get off the floor." But sometimes I just go into this mental state.'

With the video complete, Gaga was now ready to unleash her wares on the great American public and hope they'd fall in love with her and the song, as everyone around her already had. But she knew it wasn't going to be easy, as her brand of music was very different to anything that was going on in the charts at the time. So first up, she decided to play the Miami Winter Music Conference. While it was basically a wild weekend of clubbing and performers and DJs showcasing what they did best, it was also a place where people got noticed and, more importantly, talked about – just what an up-and-coming young artist needed.

Joined by her two dancers Dina and Pepper, Gaga put on a show on the rooftop of the Raleigh Hotel that had the assembled journalists scratching their heads. The song seemed pretty run-of-the mill to them – electro cool, the kind of boppy sound that was bubbling up in the UK – but seeing Gaga strut her stuff in nude tights, ankle boots, mirror-tiled 'disco panties' and a leotard left them feeling bemused. Kicking off with 'Beautiful, Dirty, Rich', the singer ground across the rooftop trailed by her two dancers, arms flailing, trying to engage the crowd. Her performance was strong and confident yet, on a video clip of it posted on YouTube, the crowd appear to be nonplussed. Even when 'Paparazzi' rang out, few of those standing around seemed to be too excited. Or perhaps the journos were just a bit too cool to freak out in the afternoon sun with a cameraman filming away. However, by the end of the set, once she had pulled out the big gun that was 'Just Dance', she had them captivated. Her mix of catchy melodies, strong vocals and unforgettable styling ensured that she was ingrained in their minds.

The rest of her stay in Miami saw her play a few gay clubs and celebrate her twenty-second birthday. But despite her ever-growing confidence that she was about to conquer the world, she would soon discover that it was going to be harder than she thought.

Chapter 14:

The Struggle for Acceptance

With the single now properly released, Gaga and her record company suddenly hit an unexpected wall. Despite reviewers giving the song a positive reception, they were finding it very hard for people actually to hear the track, which of course is paramount for a new artist. Radio stations told them that the song wasn't right for their playlists. 'They would say, "This is too racy, too dance-orientated, too underground. It's not marketable,"' she told the *Independent*. 'And I would say, "My name is Lady Gaga, I've been on the music scene for years and I'm telling you this is what's next."'

Although she may have been right about the future, she was being rebuffed by radio stations that were hooked on the joyous pop sounds of songs like Katy Perry's cheeky 'I Kissed A Girl'. Gaga understood that 'Just Dance' wasn't a typical radio track. But she didn't care. She knew that eventually this supposedly underground track would cross over to the mainstream. But when?

She wasn't put off by the lacklustre reaction of the radio stations. In fact, if anything, it spurred her on even more. After all, she was used to hard work, having trawled the Lower East Side clubs back in the day just to get known. Now, with a record to sell, she knew she had to work harder than ever.

And so her TV pluggers set about trying to get her on as many shows as possible. Fortunately, her distinctive look made her the perfect artist to dazzle on screen. Kicking off her run of spots was a PA at the NewNowNext Awards on the Logo channel, whose audience was primarily gay. Gaga went down a storm and she was delighted with the reaction, in particular from fellow guest – and one of Gaga's musical heroes – Cyndi Lauper. 'You look great,' Cyndi said, as they bumped into each other behind the scenes. 'Take no prisoners.' Gaga, who was normally ice cool, was so excited about meeting a legend whose songs she had sung as a kid that she could barely speak.

After this, more TV appearances were offered, including a spot on the Fox reality show *So You Think You Can Dance*, presented by Cat Deeley. Despite the show being prime-time and family-centric, producers took a risk on the singer and their gamble paid off. Within seconds of appearing on screen, Lady Gaga made viewers sit up as they tried to take in what they were seeing. Gaga looked like no other pop star on the market. Wearing a skimpy leotard, poker-straight, fringed, bleach-blonde hair, and LCD specs that displayed the words 'POP MUSIC WILL NEVER BE LOWBROW', she effortlessly performed 'Just Dance' with some of the contestants.

Word among the TV industry soon spread and more and more high-profile shows, among them *The Tonight Show With Jay Leno* and *Jimmy Kimmel Live*, took notice and booked her. But one of her most exciting appearances was on *The Ellen DeGeneres Show*. For years, Gaga had been a massive fan of the former comedian and sitcom star because she had pushed so many boundaries. What Gaga loved most about Ellen was that she had changed the way the public felt about gay people when she sensationally came out on her sitcom in 1997, at a time when most big stars preferred to stay in the closet. The coming-out episode was seen as highly controversial at the time and the lead up to transmission saw advertisers pull commercials from the show and religious groups up in arms. When the episode finally aired, it attracted record ratings and Ellen made the cover of *Time* magazine. Although the series came to an end shortly afterwards, Ellen fast became accepted by the mainstream, resulting in her being chosen to host the 2007 Oscars and eventually her own hugely successful chat show.

To Gaga, Ellen was therefore something of an inspiration, so when she finally sat down with her onstage, she was visibly thrilled to have met one of her idols. 'I love you so much,' she gushed at a smiling DeGeneres in a later meeting. 'It means more to me to be on this show than anywhere else. I look up to you so thank you for having me. You're an inspiration to women and the gay community.' All Ellen could say in return was a dry, 'I thought I liked you before, now I like you more.'

Gaga's TV appearances helped to give the record a push, but it was probably the club scene that did most to give the song the airing it needed. Backed by her dancers, Gaga would travel across the country and play several shows a night. Of course, going back home to New York was one of the highlights of her promotional tour. Although she caught up with friends at her usual old haunts, she also targeted the gay market by playing outrageous shows at the Pink Elephant, Tenjune, and Mansoon. By the time she got to play New York's premier gay club, Splash, it was all she could do not to jump into the crowd herself. 'I wanted to be on E,' she told *HX* magazine. 'When I play gay clubs, it's like I'm playing for my friends: they get it and understand what I am trying to say. They have a very open mind about art, pop and commercial music.'

Needless to say, it was the gay market that really took Gaga to their hearts, and slowly 'Just Dance' began to make headway on the dance charts. 'Dance in the gay community is this subculture of celebration and fun,' she told *HX* magazine. 'I draw lots of inspiration from the gay community, in an almost subconscious way so it's ingrained in me now. It's so joyful. Sometimes I say, as long as it's gay, just make sure it's gay – like for the video or for the mix on something or the clothing, I say as long as it's gay, it's good.'

Unsurprisingly she was invited to perform at the San Francisco Gay Pride, where she went down a storm. The music was perfectly suited to the club-loving crowd, whose musical ears were always looking for the latest, coolest, most cutting-edge sounds. Who cared that the suits at the radio stations were taking their time to fall in love with her, when she had grassroots fans coming out to see her? And she knew how to please her fans. Stepping out onstage as she closed the event, she said: 'Thank you, California, for legalizing gay marriage. It's about time.' The audience knew how to show their appreciation. 'The whole show was running behind so the city shut me off during "Just Dance" because it's like $10,000 a minute if they don't cut you off,' she revealed in an interview several years later. 'My mic went out, the music went off and all my gay boyfriends just sang it back to me. It was the sweetest, most amazing moment.' (www.fabmagazine.com)

While to some her gushing pro-gay stance could have sounded like a calculated marketing ploy to win over new fans, her target market lapped it up, while she was at pains to assure them that she felt an affinity with the gay community. 'I never really decided to become this kind of artist,' she told GayWired.com. 'It's just who I became and I think it's a result of my lifestyle. Just hanging out with people who are gay, transgendered or cross-dressing males and females.'

Notoriously camp gossip blogger Perez Hilton, who was well respected for his showbiz nous and ability to spot future stars, had had his eye on Gaga for some time. Swiftly, he invited her to headline the bill for his Independence Day bash at the Privé nightclub in Las Vegas. Bearing in mind that his blog at the time was one of the most popular on the planet, his coverage of the event and his exuberant raving about Lady Gaga meant that all of a sudden she was being read about from London to Tokyo.

A week or so later, Gaga played one of her biggest audiences yet at the Miss Universe 2008 pageant in Vietnam during the Swimsuit Top 15 segment. Ironically, despite her penchant for not bothering to wear trousers, this time Gaga chose to wrap herself up in a skintight PVC catsuit, with a yellow shoulder-padded jacket. The performance saw her step aside midway through the song so that the wannabe beauty queens could strut their stuff on the stage. The next day, Gaga's MySpace page was inundated with 'friend' requests.

After the show, Gaga looked back at her performance with pride. 'I thought it looked amazing!' she told The Back Building. 'I'm graphic and fashion-forward and then you have the Miss Universe pageant which is totally devoid of any fashion at all. It's purely about accentuating their bodies. Popjustice wrote something about it and said, "That is just the kind of trivial post-feminist performance that Madonna would have enjoyed watching." Pageants are seen as very chauvinistic in terms of womanhood. What I do is very boyish in a way. It has a lot of balls. It's not pretty. It's quite strange. It was a nice dichotomy.' (www.thebackbuilding.tumblr.com)

Coasting a wave of growing popularity, Gaga then accepted an invitation to join German fashion designer Michael Michalsky at his show at the Uferhallen Mercedes-Benz Fashion Week in Berlin. The canny fashion guru recognized that Gaga was on the tip of becoming the next big thing and insisted that she walk the red carpet and sit in the front row.

Michael's conviction that Gaga would cause a sensation was borne out. When Gaga stepped on to the red carpet wearing a bright yellow ribbon dress and red pointy-shouldered jacket the paparazzi went wild, demanding to know who she was. As she took her seat inside, she knew that, despite her single still hovering around the lower regions of the *Billboard* chart, true success was within touching distance.

Chapter 15:
The Fame – At Last

It's all well and good releasing a great pop record, but if no one gets to hear it, then you might as well not have made it in the first place. Although 'Just Dance' had hit number 2 in the Hot Dance Airplay and Hot Dance Club Play charts, it was still only barely making a mark on the mainstream pop chart.

No doubt using the pop-star models of yesteryear, Gaga had to ensure that every interview she gave made an impact so that people sat up and took notice. Of course, with her straight-talking ways, this would be a pretty easy task for her.

And when an interview with her was published in gay monthly *HX* magazine, the mainstream press started to pay attention. When asked if she was as boy crazy as she appeared to be in her songs, she laughed, 'Yeah, I'm girl crazy too. It really depends where I am. I love men, I love women, I love sex.'

To some it might have seemed like a stage-managed shock quip to cause controversy, as Madonna had done many times before, but Gaga was adamant that she was bisexual. 'I don't really consider sexual orientation in general,' she continued. 'It's like people are born the way they are.'

When pressed on whether she was seeing either a man or a woman at that moment, Gaga proved to be less forthcoming. 'I'm so enveloped in my work, its hard to find people that are supportive of your art and don't want to take your time away from it. A lot of times boyfriends and girlfriends get jealous and want all your attention and I don't really have the time for it.'

Of course, revelations like this aren't quite as shocking nowadays as when Ellen DeGeneres came out on her show. But still, there was something mildly titillating to male readers, in particular in the mainstream, that this sexy, free-thinking pop star was up for anything, fulfilling many heterosexual males' fantasies of a woman who swings both ways. Gaga's admission also worked for her male gay fans, as well as drawing in a lesbian audience, a group that was rarely openly courted by mainstream pop acts.

And if anyone felt that she was sharing her gay credentials as a way of trying to sell a record, as some had begun to think, Gaga had an answer. 'I don't want to be seen as using the gay community to look edgy,' she told Toronto's *Fab* magazine. 'I'm a free sexual woman and I like what I like. I don't want people to write about me because it feels like I'm saying it because I am trying to be edgy or underground.'

Luckily for Gaga her gay fans understood where she was coming from, and her newly acquired pal Perez Hilton was only too pleased to welcome her to the gaybourhood.

Meanwhile Gaga, never backwards in coming forwards, continued to delight interviewers with her frank admissions. When she was asked by *Fab* magazine the strangest place where she had ever had sex, she didn't even attempt to deflect the question. Instead she cheerfully announced she had enjoyed some wild sex in the back of a moving New York taxi. 'Sneaky sex is the best,' she purred. 'It's always fun to do things that are sneaky.'

If that wasn't enough, in another interview (with the *Independent*'s *Magazine*) she revealed that when she bedded a suitor, she would always leave them an eyelash on the pillow the next morning as a kind of souvenir. Perhaps a case of TMI? It was becoming clear that Gaga was untroubled by boundaries. But it came as no surprise – she had always been pretty open about the fact she wasn't scared to talk about taboos. 'Every artist plays on sex,' she admitted in a TV interview in Norway. 'It's just the context and we play on it differently. I'm a free woman, so I play on sex freely. But I am not the first pop artist to play on sex.'

Around this time, 'Just Dance' entered the *Billboard* chart at 76, and was already a Top 40 hit in Australia. Things were beginning to take off and Gaga hoped that the release of *The Fame* on 19 August in Canada would finally give her the push she needed.

Holding the final version of the album in her hands was a dream come true for Gaga. In the sleeve notes, she thanked all those who had helped her along the way, in particular Vincent Herbert. She also thanked her mom and dad for teaching her the 'importance of family and showing me the value of always sitting down to dinner together – and never taking a bite till everyone was present'. Gaga also paid tribute to aunt Joanne, her father's sister who had died before she was born, by including a poem of hers in the sleeve notes. 'I always felt a very strong connection to her,' she told a San Francisco radio station. 'For whatever reason, I believe that I have two hearts and in some way my life and this music is meant to finish up the rest of life that she did not get to live. So for me my motivation is to fulfil the destiny of Joanne.'

Once again she embarked on lengthy promotional tour of the US. Fortunately, the reviewers welcomed the new record with open arms. Matthew Chisling from AllMusic.com wrote: 'Fuelled by heavy dance tracks and popping electronic beats, *The Fame* is a well-crafted sampling of feisty anti-pop in high quality. Lady Gaga pulls out all the stops on *The Fame*, injecting hard-hitting synthesizers and crashing slicks and grooves. From its opening track until it closes, *The Fame* fails to come up short on funky sounds to amuse fans of this dance genre.'

Mikael Wood of *Entertainment Weekly* graded the album B–, saying that *The Fame* was 'remarkably (and exhaustingly) pure in its vision of a world in which nothing trumps being Beautiful, Dirty, Rich. In this economy, though, her high-times escapism has its charms.'

However, not all reviews were positive. Sal Cinquemani from *Slant* compared Gaga's vocals to Gwen Stefani's but cruelly sniped: 'Gaga's lyrics alternate between cheap and nonsensical drivel, and her vocal performances are uneven at best. The songs that work, including "Poker Face", "Starstruck", "Paper Gangsta" and "Summerboy", rest almost solely on their snappy production and sing-along hooks.'

Sarah Rodman from the *Boston Globe* said that 'Lady GaGa's frothy disco confections could easily be mistaken for the mindless booty bait dangled by, say, the Pussycat Dolls. But listen a little closer to the sly, snarky lyrics and glam grooves on this feisty debut and you'll hear that this former downtown New York spice girl has at least a few things on her dirty mind.'

But Gaga took all the reviews on the chin. Sure she was upset if people didn't get what she was trying to say, but she knew that she would never please everyone. 'I get tired of reading reviews [from] people who say my work is all about shallow bullsh★t,' Gaga told SongwriterUniverse.com. 'I talked to one of my good friends, Perez Hilton, about my record. He said, "Don't take this the wrong way, but you write really deep intelligent lyrics with shallow concepts." Perez is very intelligent and clearly listened to my record from beginning to end, and he is correct.'

Chapter 16:
Stars Go Gaga for Gaga

A couple of weeks after *The Fame* hit the shelves, Gaga unleashed 'Poker Face' as the follow-up to 'Just Dance', which was still lingering around the middle of the *Billboard* charts. To some fans and critics, the song was more edgy and satisfying than its predecessor and the video – shot by Ray Kay – that accompanied it, and which emerged a month or two later, looked a lot glossier. Shot at a luxury mansion on online gambling firm Bwin's poker resort, Poker Island, Gaga emerges from a huge pool wearing a mirrored mask and a black leotard, followed by her real-life Great Danes Lava and Rumpus. The rest of the video sees Gaga partaking in a good-natured game of strip poker (featuring Space Cowboy), dancing in an electric-blue space-suit bikini, joining in a PG-13 orgy and draping herself across a rather attractive and scantily clad male model. When she watched the video back, Gaga was impressed with the results. 'I knew I wanted it sexy,' she said on a video blog on her website, 'so I thought no pants because that's sexy and I knew I wanted it to be futuristic. So I thought shoulder pads because that's my thing.'

But even though there was a saucy side to the video, there was a lot of laughter on the shoot as Gaga's pet pooches weren't quite as professional as the human actors taking part. Director Ray Kay remembered on MTV News: 'There were two dog trainers on each side of the shot, trying to hold the dogs down in the position they were supposed to be in but they just kept getting up or looking in the wrong direction. So actually we never got the shot in camera the way it's shown in the video. We had to combine different takes of the dogs to get the shot the way it is in the video.'

The song proved popular and once again Gaga caused a sensation whenever she performed on TV. Although its chart ascent was again another lengthy one, the tune won over many fans, including rappers Kid Cudi and Kanye West, who sampled the acoustic version of 'Poker Face' on their track 'Make Her Say' (originally called 'Poke Her Face'). Kanye admitted that he loved the song, but was particularly enamoured by the acoustic version that he had seen on YouTube. 'I could hear all the melody lines,' he said. 'On the "Poker Face" single she sings it straightforward, almost like ripping it or chanting. But this acoustic version, you hear the Broadway melodies run up and down. I was inspired by that. I wanted to sample it, I thought it was dope.' (MTV News)

When Gaga heard the new interpretation, she was over the moon. And despite her fans thinking that she would be annoyed that they had changed the tone of the record to address themes of a sexual nature, Gaga merely laughed, telling MTV News: 'A lot of my fans were like, "Kanye wrote a song and it's not about what your record is about. Your record is about gambling and this song is about dirty sex things." But that's exactly what the song is about. The record is about how I used to fantasize about women when I was with my boyfriend.'

Meanwhile, her record label was making extra efforts for Gaga to get her music heard. Up until recently, Gaga was still songwriting with the Konvict team and had been working on material for The Pussycat Dolls. Because she had become so involved with the album her label managed to get her a support slot on their Doll Domination Tour, which would travel the US toward the end of the year before moving across to Europe. Gaga wasn't stupid – she knew that The Pussycat Dolls were popular all around the globe, which meant that as support act she would be seen by hundreds of thousands of people. What a brilliant way of introducing herself to the world.

But before that, Gaga not only got asked to write songs with New Kids on the Block on their reunion album, she also landed herself a stint on their US autumn tour with Colby O'Donis and Brit singer Natasha Bedingfield. This was great news for Gaga as she had spent some of her childhood idolizing these handsome young boys. And now here she was working with them, just like she had with Britney – only this time she would be working directly with them in the studio and then joining them on the road later in the year. 'I love them,' she shamelessly gushed to the *San Francisco Chronicle*. 'I just love them so much, I can't really talk about it. When I first met them, I almost had a heart attack. It's really humbling and incredible. Donnie [Wahlberg] took a liking to my work and writing style and loved my vibe. It's been an incredible experience.'

Working with Donnie and the boys on the track 'Full Service' proved to be a dream-come-true, pinch-yourself experience for Gaga. While he may not have been the usual stringy-looking, Nikki Sixx type of guy Gaga usually went for, Donnie definitely tickled her fancy. And as it turned out, the feelings were mutual. Donnie revealed all to the *Daily Mirror* later that year: 'Lady Gaga is delicious – we got quite close. We co-wrote a song; she's very talented. I didn't have sex with her but I wouldn't say no.'

While her extensive promotional tour was alerting people to her existence, TV companies were falling over themselves to use her edgy music on their shows. Even before *The Fame* was released her label had managed to get her songs twenty-five TV and film placements. The producers of short-lived family drama *Dirty Sexy Money* asked to use 'Beautiful, Dirty, Rich' in their promo for the show. Gaga was totally up for it and, to tie in with its release as the third single, she and director Melina Matsoukas edited two versions: one as her official promo and the other one featuring clips from the soapy drama.

Meanwhile, her songs were turning up on all manner of shows like *Gossip Girl* and *The Hills*. Gaga was pleased that her work had a life beyond her fans' stereos. 'I call the record label and I'm like, "Oh my God, I didn't know the song was on that show,"' she told *Beatweeek Magazine*. 'There have been so many licences recently that I don't even hear about all of them. But that makes me feel great because it tells me that my goal, which was to analyse and reckon and struggle with ideas about pop culture, is really working because all these shows that are emblematic of modern television and modern film and modern movies and modern clubs – it's like they're all gravitating to my stuff, because I guess it's speaking to something that is very today.'

While she was still waiting for success to happen in the US, her singles and albums were more popular in other territories, in particular in Canada, where both 'Just Dance' and *The Fame* had topped the charts. When she played the Dragonfly nightclub in Niagara Falls, she couldn't contain her emotions and constantly thanked everyone in the club for buying her records.

Across the Atlantic, the Swedes were also digging Gaga and she was invited to headline the NRJ music festival in Stockholm in front of 50,000 eager fans. Shortly afterwards she appeared at the Valtifest festival in Amsterdam, where again she was warmly greeted. It was all well and good having fans in her home country, but to think that people hundreds of thousands of miles away loved her music seemed beyond belief to her. And if she thought that this was enough of an ego boost, it was nothing compared to the moment she clapped eyes on one of her pop idols performing at the MTV awards ceremony, which was taking place across the Atlantic.

Peering at Space Cowboy's laptop on the tour bus, Gaga was stunned to see pop powerhouse Christina Aguilera emerge on screen to sing a new version of her classic hit 'Genie In A Bottle' mixed with her new single 'Keeps Gettin' Better' – looking just like her. Poker-straight hair with a Gaga-esque fringe? Check! Black masquerade mask? Check! PVC black catsuit? Check! Sleazy body gyrations? Check. If Gaga hadn't known better she would have thought that she herself was actually in Hollywood at that very moment performing in front of an audience of millions. Checking online, she found the net awash with pop fans commenting on how Christina had ripped off Gaga's distinctive look. Some even suggested that the sound of her new record was very similar in style to 'Just Dance', in that it was more electro than her previous efforts. As is the way with all devoted fans, both camps got caught up in an online battle, each defending their idol to the hilt. Since Gaga had been an admirer of Aguilera when she was younger she was keen not to join in the bunfight and tried to calm things down in an interview with *Blender* magazine. 'A lot of people have been saying that she is copying my style with her new song,' she said. 'I guess it bears somewhat of a resemblance but I wouldn't say she is copying me. This type of dance music is becoming more popular and I don't blame her for wanting to make it and perform it. Her performance was great and "Keeps Gettin' Better" is a hot track!'

While Gaga was touring in Europe, she crossed the Channel to visit her spiritual home of London, where she was set to play two shows, one of which was at OMO, a gay night at what used to be the Astoria nightclub. There she treated her fans – who at this point still couldn't officially get hold of the songs (the album wouldn't be released in the UK until January 2009) – to 'LoveGame', 'Beautiful, Dirty, Rich' and 'Just Dance'. Whilst in London, she checked out some of the cool fashion areas in the capital that Lady Starlight had suggested, but because of her whirlwind schedule, she couldn't do all the sightseeing and shopping she wanted. Next she was off to Paris, where she checked out the museums and the fashion stores, before heading to Australia. Sadly for Gaga, the twenty-six hour flight wasn't very relaxing.

Partway through the journey, the pilot announced that something was wrong with one engine but urged his passengers not to panic. Of course, the words 'something wrong' and 'engine' do not normally sit well when you're thousands of feet above the ground, especially when the rate of descent was faster than normal. Afterwards Gaga admitted that she didn't cry until they reached the ground safely.

But she didn't have time to worry about her near-death experience. She had a tour schedule to stick to. Once she'd completed a sell-out gig in Sydney she was booked on to the country's leading breakfast show, *Sunrise*, for an interview and performance. However, upon arrival she realized her voice was feeling strained and arranged for the sound engineers to mix her vocals in with the backing vocals. On camera, it looked very much like she was lip-synching, and inevitably she was slated in the local press and online.

Gaga was furious. Writing on the *Sunrise* website, she hit back at the criticisms: 'I was sick the day of the show but I absolutely, 100 per cent was singing live. I have never lip-synched and never will. Even on my worst day, I never will.' She went on to tell a Danish reporter that her voice had suffered because on her promotional tour she had been performing two shows a night for a month and a half.

Because of the style of music she performed, some critics did doubt Gaga's vocal ability and some had even pointed out that she used Autotune on her songs. But Gaga had an answer. 'It's not for my voice,' she told the South Australian *Telegraph*. 'The radio is used to a certain perfection and it compresses the voice in a certain kind of way. It smooshes all of the sound together so it sounds smaller but fatter. It's not open, it's more condensed. Unless you are Duffy, where it's this extremely organic record, it's important to play into the psychology of the listener who is used to a certain sonic quality in the voice. If they don't hear that, it's not hip.'

But if she needed to prove the quality of her singing voice, her support slot on the New Kids' autumn tour would do the trick.

Chapter 17:
Ding Ding! Christina vs Gaga – Round Two

It seemed on paper that everything was going well for Gaga. She had an album of great songs in the shops, her tracks were being used on TV shows, she was landing guest spots on the best chat shows around. But for some reason, the major success she sought in the US still wasn't quite happening. Why?

She needed to find another way to share her music with the public and the New Kids tour was the perfect opportunity. The punters might not be paying to come and see her strut her stuff onstage, but once they checked her out, they would never forget her name. In order to maximize her appeal, she decided to up the ante and create an unforgettable stage show. While most support acts performed against black sheet backgrounds, Gaga was determined to put on a proper production. Of course this would cost money – but that didn't faze her. Checking out the dates of the New Kids tour, she decided that she would perform another full set at a club in whichever city they landed in and use the money raised to pay for the stage set, which would include two giant LCD screens upon which she would screen some short films while she performed. She would also get her Haus of Gaga to conjure up some spectacular new costumes and would add four hunky dancers to her troupe, dropping her female dancers Dina and Coco in the process.

Gaga caught up with the tour a few shows in, joining the boys in LA on 8 October 2008. The shows were a sell-out, but when she hit the stage the auditorium wasn't totally full, as most of the fans were in the eating and drinking areas awaiting the headline act. But as she'd hoped, the audience was intrigued by her stage act and presentation and gave her a very warm reaction when she finished. Still high from her performance, she stood in the wings and watched the headliners whip the crowd into a frenzy. She would later say their showmanship was a great inspiration to her: 'They are so cool and talented and so motivated. It's been fifteen years and they hit that f***ing stage like it's 1986!' (Helia Phoenix, *Lady Gaga: Just Dance*)

After the show, she and her team took off to San Francisco for a tour of the gay clubs, where she was met by fans from far and wide. 'I just played a show in San Francisco,' she told *Blackbook* magazine. 'It was meant to be a gay night at a club and it was not just gays. It was gays, straights, you know, men, women. It was black, it was white, it was Asian – it was everybody showing up on a gay night.'

But her most ardent fan was about to change her life completely. Perez Hilton, the self-made gossip blogger whose influence was sweeping across the globe at a ferocious rate, adored everything Gaga was doing. As an openly gay man, he recognized a kindred soul in Gaga. And she was so grateful for his support – his website at this time was read by tens of millions a day the world over – that she let him premiere the video of 'Poker Face' on his site.

By late 2008, Hilton was so influential in the media industry that when he decided to throw a party or organize a show, many of the A-list stars he had written about would clamour to get an invite. So when he asked Gaga if she would headline his One Night In New

York City gig, she jumped at the chance. The show, which took place at the Highline Ballroom, also featured a slew of support acts, such as the Dap-Kings and Gaga's pals Semi Precious Weapons, but none of them compared to the Lady herself. She put on a show that left her fans scrabbling to the front of the venue, desperate to get a closer look at the singer.

As she continued on the New Kids tour, Gaga's confidence began to grow. Online commentators were beginning to big her up and a real buzz was building around her. When the tour stopped off at Madison Square Garden on 27 October, Gaga's excitement was palpable. Not only was she performing in her favourite city, it was also the day her album was finally released in the US. To celebrate the release she agreed to perform in the Virgin Megastore in Union Square. What the fans saw that day would no doubt remain with them for the rest of their lives. Unlike most stars, who would perform very simply at a store promo, Gaga had brought along her entire stage set. Fans piled in to see her show, desperately trying to get as close to her as they could. And, of course, Gaga was only too happy to oblige. During her set, she clambered up a pole and tossed herself into the awaiting mob for a spot of crowd surfing. Amazingly no one, including Gaga herself, was hurt during this episode – which was fortunate for her as no sooner was the in-store appearance over than she was back on her tour bus to Madison Square Garden for her support slot.

Every day that passed she felt more and more excited about the way her career was going. And there was more to come. The week *The Fame* was released, it entered the charts at number 17 on the *Billboard* listings and a very respectable number 5 on the iTunes rundown. Despite the mixed reviews, it seemed the commercial success that had been eluding her was hers at last.

But still she pushed herself. She didn't want a number 17, or a number 16, she wanted a number 1 record. Was it too much to ask? In her view the only way this could be achieved was by continuing to play shows at all hours of the night, even if meant rarely getting to bed. Yet her hard work paid off, because at each show more and more people would turn up to see her, and more and more of them began to emulate her unusual style.

But if there was one person who helped give Gaga the push into the mainstream she needed it was Christina Aguilera, even though the legendary vocal powerhouse probably didn't even realize she was doing it. Ever since she had appeared on the MTV Awards a few weeks before looking decidedly Gaga, Christina had been bombarded with questions about this upcoming pop starlet. When she was asked by the *Los Angeles Times* how she felt about people accusing her of stealing Gaga's look, Christina got her manicured claws out: 'This person was just brought to my attention not too long ago. I'm not quite sure who this person is, to be honest. I don't know if it is a man or a woman. I just wasn't sure. I don't really spend time on the internet so I guess I live a little under a rock in that respect.'

Suddenly the internet forums were awash with angry music fans taking sides. Team Gaga hit out at seasoned singer Christina for being so bitchy, while Team Aguilera reckoned that this pop newbie was a wannabe with a limited future.

Christina even spoke up again in an interview with MTV about her VMA performance, claiming that her change of style was most certainly not inspired by the 'Just Dance' singer. 'I wanted to give [fans] a little sneak preview of what's to come,' she said. 'The vein of the new material is a futuristic take on what is inspiring me at the moment . . . and it's got a very pop-art feel, visually. [There's a] throwback to Andy Warhol and all the colours and vividness and bright boldness that was in that artwork. I'm a big collector of pop art and graffiti art at this point, too — D★Face and Banksy, also Roy Lichtenstein . . . and it's been very fun venturing off into that zone.' So far, so Gaga. Or so the fans thought. As the anger on the forums became more and more ferocious, Perez Hilton decided to wade in with his then considerable weight, writing on his site: 'As many of you know by now, it's obvious that Christina Aguilera has been borrowing looks from Lady Gaga. Her hair, her make-up, her outfits. Even her music is starting to sound more like Gaga's! Now she's dissing Gaga some more in another new interview! Aguilera just "laughs those comparisons off" and instead she goes on to name-drop everyone that has recently inspired her, minus Gaga. Xtina says that Sia and Goldfrapp are big inspirations for her current look and sound. Yea, right!'

Hilton then went on to ridicule Christina for 'borrowing' Gaga's terminology, as she had recently started talking about her 'pop art' inspiration – obviously key Gaga territory. The result of the spat was that every time Christina was getting a mention in the press, so too was Gaga.

Unsurprisingly as the NKOTB tour continued across the country, the fans would increasingly make it to the gigs in time to watch the support act, curious to see who had been ruffling Christina's feathers. As for Aguilera's swipe at Gaga, suggesting she wasn't sure what sex she was, Gaga took it all on the chin. 'I don't take offence to it,' she told EarSucker.com. 'I'm inspired by androgyny and David Bowie and Grace Jones.' Referring to Christina's MTV performance that had started off the feud, she added: 'The performance beared [sic] a resemblance. I don't have a look. I dress like this all the time. I have no enemies.' She also told *Fab* magazine that she didn't find Christina's comments offensive. In fact, Gaga continued to be strangely gracious, praising her pop elder. 'I happen to think Christina is extremely talented and I was always a big fan of hers when I was little. When someone calls you up and says that Christina Aguilera said something about you in the press you gotta be like, "What's going on?"'

In December 2008, Gaga accepted a slot on New York radio station Z100's annual Jingle Ball. The show featured some of the greatest pop acts around, such as Leona Lewis, Katy Perry and Rihanna. But when she arrived at Madison Square Garden, she was amazed to find out that Bruce Springsteen was backstage at the show with his kids – and they were apparently fans of hers. When her mother Cynthia, who was there, told her about it, she couldn't believe her ears. It was Bruce Springsteen, the man, the legend, whom she and her father used to listen to when she was just a kid herself. She simply couldn't believe that a man she had idolized for years was in the same room as her, asking after her. After she met him, a giddy Gaga gushed on MTV News, 'He told me I was sweet. Then I had a massive breakdown – I cried on this man's neck!'

Yes, Gaga was definitely starting to get noticed in the right places. While she hadn't let herself be drawn into a petty catfight with Christina Aguilera, she couldn't help be satisfied that as a result of the column inches surrounding the feud, in combination with her endless personal appearances, her fanbase had increased, with her MySpace following doubling up in numbers. She even joked in the US edition of *OK!* magazine that she ought to send Aguilera flowers to say thanks for the step up. 'A lot of people in America didn't know who I was until that whole thing happened,' she laughed. 'It really put me on the map in a way.'

Gaga was also pleased that her fans and the world in general were noticing a key factor that made her unique: her sense of style. While her outlandish outfits and masks may have made some people baulk, they definitely made them remember her. This concept was ingrained in her from her days with Lady Starlight, who had encouraged her to turn each gig into performance art. Helped by Matty and her Haus of Gaga, she dazzled onstage in outfits that most people had never seen before.

From the first, Gaga was clear that she wanted to push the boundaries of fashion. She wanted to be perceived as a pop star, which meant she had to look like a pop star. And her thinking was making an impact. Suddenly, other stars started wearing fashion-forward outfits on the red carpet. Gone were simple gowns – instead young celebs rocked up to events in more and more eccentric garb.

The Lady Gaga effect was well under way.

Chapter 18:
Gaga Hits the Road

If the idea that her style was beginning to permeate the mainstream wasn't enough to put a smile on Gaga's face, the news that her single 'Just Dance' had been nominated for a Best Dance Grammy most certainly would. What's more, she was battling it out against top stars like Daft Punk, Rihanna and her pop idol, Madonna.

But Gaga would have to wait until February to find out if she stood a chance of winning her first prestigious award. For the time being, she was focused on travelling around Europe supporting the Pussycat Dolls on tour, which would coincide with the release of *The Fame* in the UK. She was also celebrating the news that 'Just Dance' had finally reached number 3 in the *Billboard* Christmas chart, just behind Beyoncé's 'Single Ladies' and Rihanna and TI's hit 'Live Your Life'.

Gaga capped off 2008 with a special New Year show at the historic Webster Hall in New York. There she was joined by all her friends for the massive bash, which would last until the very early hours of the morning. The booze flowed, 100,000 balloons were set up in the ceiling so they could be dropped at midnight and the mood was high. Stepping out on to the stage, Gaga was clearly emotional. Her life over the past twelve months had changed completely. Back in January she was fresh off the plane from New York, hungover but keen to start work on the next stage of her pop career. Now almost a year on, she'd toured the country, had a spat with a pop legend and achieved major commercial success.

'One year ago today,' she said, 'on New Year's, I was on top of a bar in quite a leathered condition, go-go dancing on the Lower East Side for money. And now I'm ringing in the new season with all you people.'

After her energetic performance, the balloons were freed and the New Year was welcomed in. A week later, as Gaga prepared for the Pussycat Dolls tour, news reached her that – eight months after its initial release – 'Just Dance' had finally reached the number 1 spot in the US! That she was thrilled was an understatement. But more was to come. Just as her good news was sinking in, she received a phone call to inform her that the single had also just topped the charts in the UK, knocking Alexandra Burke's Christmas number 1 'Hallelujah' off the top spot and selling more in downloads alone. Unable to contain her joy, Gaga and burst into tears. Meanwhile, 'Poker Face' was smashing its way up the charts in Sweden and Australia. Gaga-mania was spreading across the world like a virus.

But celebration had to be set aside for the time being. There was no time to draw breath. Instead, she started working on the choreography for the Pussycat Dolls tour with renowned creative director Laurieann Gibson, recorded some pared-down versions of album tracks for a future EP and shot two videos for the tracks 'Eh, Eh' and 'LoveGame' with director Joseph Kahn, who had worked with Britney on the über-cool video for 'Toxic'.

The video for 'Eh, Eh', possibly the most cheesy and Europop-sounding of all Gaga's tracks, is bright, colourful and frothy. Set in New York, it shows Gaga strolling along a street in a bright turquoise leotard with some girlfriends and preparing dinner for a 'boyfriend' in her underwear. 'I wanted to show a different side of myself, perhaps a more domestic girly side,' she told PopEater.com. 'And I wanted to create beautiful, stunning 1950s futuristic fashion imagery that would burn holes in everyone's brains.' Although the fashions were not quite as avant-garde as we would see later, the outfits were truly dazzling. The skimpy bra and panties teamed with bright cerise stilettoes was definitely an image not easily forgotten, but neither was the yellow flower dress worn during the closing stages of the video.

The 'LoveGame' video was also very New York-centric, but by contrast offered a much darker image of the city. In it, Gaga is seen cruising the subways with her homies. The outfits she wears, which she says were influenced by Michael Jackson's classic 'Bad' video, definitely do show signs of developing an eccentric twist; in one scene she is wearing a PVC leotard that leaves very little to the imagination, then in another she wears a metal-studded pair of panties with a leather jacket. In a third scene she appears almost naked while elsewhere she is wearing a mesh visor and dancing with her face sprinkled with sparkles. Gaga loved making the film, admitting on ew.com PopWatch: 'I wanted to have that big giant dance video moment. I wanted to be plastic, beautiful, sweaty, tar on the floor, bad ass boys, but when you get close, the look in everybody's eyes was f***ing honest and scary.' She also had a blast on the shoot as she and one of the male dancers, Speedy, had formed a rather tight bond.

Once filming had wrapped, she flew over to the UK to catch up with the Pussycat Dolls. When she arrived at Heathrow, she was stunned to find paps waiting for her. But she'd had a number 1 single; she'd have to get used to being recognized.

In fact, during her stay, and thanks to her dangerously revealing outfits, she and the paparazzi became partners-in-crime in London. If they wanted a spectacle, she didn't mind giving it to them. After all, it could only help her to achieve the worldwide fame she had sought for so long. So, increasingly when Gaga was seen out and about, her outfits would become more and more outrageous, captivating

The many faces of Gaga: (*top left*) with her father at the 52nd annual GRAMMY Awards in 2010; (*top right*) sporting a fake wound at the Fontainebleau Miami Beach hotel on New Year's Eve 2009; (*below*) meeting the Queen at the Royal Variety Performance in 2009.

(*right*) With Sharon Osbourne and Cyndi Lauper at the MAC VIVA GLAM launch in 2010.

(*below*) Showcasing another china teacup and some impressive headgear while promoting her single 'Telephone' on *Friday Night With Jonathan Ross* in March 2010.

(*top right*) Rock and pop legends past and present: Gaga onstage with (*l-r*) Sting, Debbie Harry, Elton John, Dame Shirley Bassey and Bruce Springsteen.

(*right*) Commanding huge audiences on her Monster Ball Tour in July 2010.

(*far right*) Crowd-surfing during the 2010 Lollapalooza Festival in Chicago.

(*left and below*) Lady Gaga's art knows no bounds: onstage in Milan in 2010 and Cumbria, Britain in 2011.

(*top far left*) Winning the award for the best pop video for 'Bad Romance' at the 2010 MTV Video Music Awards.

(*top left*) The headline-grabbing meat dress Gaga wore to the same ceremony. The outfit was voted *Time* magazine's top fashion statement of 2010.

(*left*) Honouring John Lennon's seventieth birthday onstage with Yoko Ono in October 2010.

The Haus of Gaga works its magic: debuting an array of eye-catching outfits in 2011.

(*top left*) Lady Gaga dressed up as her drag king alter ego Joe Calderone at 2011's MTV Music Awards.

(*top right*) Arriving in style: Lady Gaga emerges from a giant perfume bottle at the Macy's launch of her own scent 'Fame' in 2012.

(*left*) With Mick Jagger when she joined The Rolling Stones on tour in 2012 for one night only.

Superstar: Performing at the 2011 MTV Europe Music Awards in Belfast, Northern Ireland. Lady Gaga's position at the pinnacle of pop is cemented.

a public that had not experienced a pop star quite as eccentric since David Bowie and the glam rockers of the seventies.

Before joining the Doll Domination Tour, Gaga appeared at London's G-A-Y club, which by now had moved to Heaven. The night was a sell-out, with a queue stretching around the block. Before she appeared onstage, Gaga screened one of her 'crevettes' – short art films used as introductions to her live shows (*crevette* means 'shrimp' in French) – in which she is seen as 'Candy Warhol' speaking about having her brain removed. Whether the euphoric clientele paid any attention to the oddball film is anyone's guess, as most of the revellers were screaming and cheering so loudly the soundtrack was barely audible. When she finally made it onstage and performed her set, the baying crowd all but tore the roof off.

Without a doubt, Gaga had become the darling of the British press. Tabloid hacks were desperate to print pictures of her in varying states of undress (which Gaga only encouraged by wearing the skimpiest of garments), and to find any stories they could on this newly formed superstar. The press had a field day writing about how the Pussycat Dolls were livid that Gaga was eclipsing their tour and attracting all the headlines away from them. But Nicole Scherzinger and the girls laughed off the reports and said they were excited to have Lady Gaga joining them, as she was 'fresh, creative, talented and exciting'.

Former Doll Kimberly Wyatt looks back at that time with great fondness and admits that she is proud that they were partly responsible for introducing Gaga to the rest of the world.

'I think we all knew that Gaga was someone to watch,' Kimberly recalled (in an interview with the author). 'We knew a bit about her because she was signed to Interscope Records and her first gig was writing songs for the Dolls, one of them being "Just Dance", which was a song she wrote for us that we didn't end up recording and that took her to massive success. I remember performing at the O2 and some of us would sneak out and try and watch her show before it was time for us to go on and then you'd see people with the Gaga lightning bolt on their faces and dressing up as Gaga and we knew almost immediately that this girl was going to be massive and we were definitely right.'

Kimberly also remembered (interview with the author) how Gaga was always asking the girls questions about the music business. 'We were doing a gig in Philadelphia together in a club and she came barging into our room and asking us for tips on singing live for an entire show and how we dance the way we do and trying to ask us about the industry really. Then the next time we saw her she was just taking everything on board and really performing like a crazy madwoman . . . You see her behind the scenes on the phone at all times being the creative hero in her own life and calling the shots and coming up with these ideas and starting her own company; you see that she's building an empire by herself. She is the brains and the operation behind the Lady Gaga industry. Massive respect to her that she's gotten that chance and she's continuing to take it to such great heights. She's a genius songwriter.'

Denying rumours that the girls were jealous of Gaga's growing popularity, Kimberly said, 'It's not my place to speak for anyone else but I would say that we were just really proud of her and, speaking for myself, we wanted to see her succeed. I just think she's fantastic at what she does and she works really hard so to think that we were a bit of a platform for her to get out there to meet the success that she has now is kinda mindblowing!'

Whether or not Kimberly and her bandmates actually meant it, the Dolls were right to stay on Gaga's good side. Not only did 'Just Dance' enjoy a week at number 1, 'Poker Face' entered the chart the same week at around number 30 and *The Fame* burst on to the album chart at number 3.

In February of that year, Gaga fulfilled another dream when she performed alongside the Pet Shop Boys at the Brit Awards. The group, who had been honoured with a Lifetime Contribution to Music Award, had asked Gaga to join them on the song 'What

Have I Done To Deserve This?' She also duetted with Brandon Flowers on the PSB track 'West End Girls'. After the show, Neil Tennant explained how the collaboration had come about. 'At the beginning of the year we were thinking of looking for a fabulous girl singer to sing the Dusty [Springfield] part of "What Have I Done To Deserve This?" And then miraculously at number 1 was the record "Just Dance" by Lady Gaga and we thought, "That's her."' (Interview at the Brit Awards, ITV2)

Gaga was coasting a wave, and enjoying every single minute. But her workload – her tour schedule meant she was occasionally performing four shows a night – was beginning to take its toll on her and rumours of her burning out riddled the gossip columns. Still, she was just pleased that she was finally making her mark. 'It's just so amazing to see how powerful music is,' she said in one of her blogs for her *Transmission Gagavision* web series. 'You don't even realize it until you're out here and doing it. I was just in my car and my song came on the radio. It's just amazing to see everything coming together.'

In fact, despite all the hard work she was putting in, she admitted to *Billboard* that she was the happiest she'd ever been. 'It's required a tremendous amount of heart and faith and really believing. I really love what I do so much. I always say that I'm not waiting for some lump of cash so I can buy my beach house – I'm living my dream now.'

But in spite of everything that was happening around her, she still had one dream left to fulfil. She wanted to headline her own tour. And during a break in the Pussycat Dolls tour, she was determined to make that dream come true.

Chapter 19:
Going It Alone

When she had played the dingy bars on the Lower East Side, Gaga had performed as if she were playing to a crowd of thousands. In reality, she was lucky if there were fifty or so people in the room, and even more fortunate if they actually bothered to pay any attention. Now Gaga's dream was to take her show on the road and play to thousands of eager fans who would hang on her every word.

As she had discovered on the recent Pussycat Dolls tour, the audiences were now beginning to get what she did. She was, she realized, finally starting to experience what it felt like to be a real star. Of course, most of the crowds who watched her strut her stuff on these supporting tours had paid their ticket money to see the headline act and had only stumbled across her by default, but she was aware that there were a growing number who had come to see her in particular.

So Gaga felt ready to tour. Her singles were topping the charts worldwide, her album was flying out of the shops – now she felt it was time for that all-important headline tour, during which she could thank all those wonderful fans who had taken her to their hearts.

And so the Fame Ball Tour was imagined. It would of course be a work of performance art. Together with her Haus of Gaga team, she set about working on the production – and with her mind full of ideas, it would be a show like nothing on earth. 'I am so excited about this tour,' she told *Rolling Stone* magazine. 'This is so different from anything you have seen from me in the past year!'

And she wasn't exaggerating. In comparison to her recent support stints, this tour would be even more of a visual treat. In the weeks leading up to the first show, which was due to take place at the House of Blues in San Diego on 12 March 2009, Gaga played it cool, initially refusing to reveal too many details and whipping fans and journalists into a foaming frenzy of excitement.

Of course, as Gaga was so excited about her forthcoming jaunt, she couldn't keep quiet for long and soon she started offering revealing glimpses of the preparations: 'This is going to be like the ultimate creative orgasm for me 'cos I'm ready to move on. I'm not restricted to a certain structure for my show any more. No limitations, I'm free. I want to have a clear schedule of the dimensions for each venue so that we can properly execute all the technology and visuals. I need to mentally prepare days in advance if things are going to be taken out; otherwise I won't have a good show. Every show is going to be an A-show by the time I'm done screaming at everyone – "Hang it! Hang everything! Find a place to hang it!" That's going to be my motto.'

She went on to explain to MTV what her fans could expect from the shows: 'It's not really a tour, it's more of a travelling party. I want it to be an experience from the minute you walk in the door to the minute I begin to sing. And when it's all over everyone's going to press rewind and live it again. It's going to be like you are walking into New York circa 1974; there's an art installation in the lobby, a DJ spinning your favourite records and the most haunting performance you've ever seen onstage.'

She went on to say: 'The Ball is so important. I want so much to make every Depression dollar that everyone spends on my show worth it. And yeah, I'm paying a lot for it – out of my own pocket. But that's OK, I don't care about money!'

And to prove that, she also decided that a share of the ticket prices would be donated to worthy causes, such as schools in the US that had been affected by budget cuts.

When the tour finally kicked off, fans were in no doubt about how much they loved what they saw. As expected it was typical Gaga and then some. They lapped up the opening crevette entitled *The Heart*, in which her alter ego Candy Warhol announced, 'I am Lady Gaga and this is my Haus!' Then they went totally wild as the star herself – wearing a futuristic bubble-dress that was inspired by a Hussein Chalayan dress that she'd seen a few months before – launched into her hit 'Paparazzi', surrounded by an army of dancers. The rest of the show followed suit, punctuating her album tracks with video installations. And of course, the costume changes were a sight to behold, with Gaga sporting spectacular garments that offered her fans a glimpse of the fashion of the future, mixing black geometric dresses with others boasting elaborate accessories, a sculpted prom dress and an origami dress that she had worn a couple of years earlier.

While the shows went down a storm with her fans, the critics were divided. Most were positive, with both the *Chicago Tribune* and the *Hollywood Reporter* praising her for commanding the stage, 'with a royal air' said the latter. However, there were some – usually considerably less successful – stars who were only too keen to share their rather negative reactions. Alan Donohoe, front man of rock band The Rakes, savaged Gaga, suggesting she dressed like a hooker. 'I think she's terrible and really ugly,' he said in an interview in which he was plugging his group's latest album. 'I hate her.'

But for every jealous star, there were others who truly appreciated that a superstar was emerging. R&B sensation Ne-Yo was smitten with the singer and gushed to the *Daily Star* in the UK: 'I have never been so excited about a pop artist before. She has it all. Being yourself is what makes an artist. You should nurture what you've got. She epitomizes what artistry is about. She makes no apologies for who she is.'

If Gaga wasn't already pleased that her music and persona were winning over the record buyers of the world, then the fact she was attracting the interest of the hard-to-impress celebrities tickled her even more. When her Fame Ball hit LA's Wiltern Theater, the likes of Kelly Osbourne, LeAnn Rimes and a certain Mr Kanye West were spotted enjoying the show. Yet even the fact that she was 'celeb hot' meant little in comparison to the moment at the end of the show when her biggest supporter, Perez Hilton, stepped out onstage to present her with a special gift to celebrate the fact that her single 'Just Dance' had sold over 3 million copies worldwide. Not bad for a song that had taken some eight months to climb the US chart!

Overwhelmed by the news, Gaga broke down in tears and thanked the crowd of proud fans, telling them 'I f***ing love you!' as she left the stage.

And the good news kept rolling. Over in the UK, 'Poker Face' was topping the chart in the same week her album *The Fame* reached the top spot – giving her the rare honour of topping both charts simultaneously. Similarly, 'Just Dance' was also fast becoming the biggest-selling single in the UK, achieving figures of over 550,000 copies.

But it wasn't just her music that was captivating everyone. Gaga's eccentric style of dress was also beginning to inspire the jaded world of celebrities, who all of sudden seemed to decide it was a good time to take a risk with their wardrobes. Even straitlaced Paris Hilton was spotted pounding the streets dressed all in black with a headband and ruby-red lips. Seeing the funny side of this homage Gaga jokingly reprimanded her, blogging: 'Get your own style, Hilly.'

Despite the whirlwind of interest swirling around her, Gaga

was continuing to focus on her work. Next up was making the promo video for her next single 'Paparazzi'. As her success grew, her record label was more inclined to bow to her demands – so for this video she decided that she wanted to produce a short film. With Swedish director Jonas Åkerlund at the helm, the video co-starred fellow Scandinavian Alexander Skarsgård as the boyfriend of Gaga, who plays a starlet who is hounded by the paps. In one scene, the boyfriend leads Gaga out on to the balcony where they start making out. When she sees some camera-ready paps in some nearby bushes below and realizes that her boyfriend is in cahoots with the snappers, they fight, resulting in her hitting him over the head with a bottle, to which he responds by hurling her over the edge of the balcony. The fall leaves Gaga temporarily in a wheelchair, so the press gleefully proclaims that her career is over. But Gaga has other ideas, gets back with her boyfriend and swiftly poisons him. The result? Gaga is back in the headlines. The video ends with her posing for police mugshots as if they were paparazzi shots. Of course, at the time of the video's release the latest celeb trend appeared to be stars getting arrested, so the 'Paparazzi' clip was seen by many as a critique of the culture of celebrities who sought notoriety to increase their media value.

The imagery of the video was very different to Gaga's previous videos and it was clear that the budgets were rather more sizeable. Jonas Åkerlund's wife Bea had been brought in to style the shoot and had pulled in outfits from designers such as Thierry Mugler, Dior, D&G, Chanel, Boudicca and Boy London. Not only that, but Gaga got to live every girl's dream of wearing the most luxurious diamond bracelets, courtesy of Loree Rodkin, which were worth around $100,000 (£63,000).

Although the shoot ran smoothly, it was reported at the time that Gaga's then-boyfriend Speedy – a guy she had met a few months before on the set of 'LoveGame' – wasn't happy about a scene in which she makes out with triplets from Swedish band Snake of

Eden. According to the tittle-tattle, Speedy furiously stormed on set, yelling at her. As a result of this public display, Gaga swiftly ended her relationship with him, knowing that she was unable to carry on a relationship with a man who would so easily get jealous.

In any case, perhaps the writing was already on the wall for their relationship. Although she was never one to open up about her personal life, she did once let slip, in an interview with the *Independent*, where he had stood in her busy life. 'Speedy means a lot to me, but my music's not going to wake me up tomorrow morning and tell me it doesn't love me any more. So I'm content with my solitude, I'm OK with being alone – I choose to have someone in my life when I can.'

But while her personal life was in turmoil, her professional life continued to go from strength to strength, as her album sales were boosted by an appearance on *American Idol*, which was the perfect showcase for her talents. The *New York Times* described it as 'five of the oddest minutes in that show's history'. Not only that, 'Poker Face' became her second US chart-topper, which made Gaga the first artists in over ten years to have her first two hits reach pole position in the US. Truly her star was in the ascendant.

Chapter 20:
Storm in a China Teacup

By this stage, Gaga was becoming as famous for her avant-garde style of dress as she was her music. And she was loving it. Wherever she went, she knew the paps weren't too far away, which meant that her image was constantly in the public arena. She knew that her fans adored the way she dressed and she said on numerous occasions that she wanted to make sure that they would only ever see her as Gaga. She didn't want to be the type of celeb who was snapped in sweatpants and no make-up. She wanted to emulate those great stars of the past who were always 'on'. 'This is showbiz for me,' she would later tell *Rolling Stone* magazine. 'If I were to ever, God forbid, get hurt onstage and my fans were screaming outside the hospital, waiting for me, I'd come out as Gaga. I wouldn't come out in sweatshirts. And that's what Michael Jackson did. Michael got burned and he lifted that glittered glove so damn high so his fans could see him, because he was in the art of showbusiness.' She added: 'I don't want people to see I'm a human being. I don't even drink water onstage in front of anybody because I want them to focus on the fantasy of the music and be transported from where they are to somewhere else. People can't do that if you're on Earth. We need to go to heaven!'

And dreaming up ways to make the press take notice came easily. In fact, she discovered along the way that carrying something as simple as a china cup was enough to create a buzz around her. When she jetted over to the UK in April, Gaga was snapped holding a china cup and saucer. Now this wouldn't have been so strange had she been leaving a café with a beverage she hadn't finished. But she wasn't – she was merely holding it as normally as she would a handbag. Interest surrounding the cup continued to grow when it was spotted again with her when she appeared on *The Jonathan Ross Show*. This was one of her first major interviews in the UK and it was clear that the renowned host was slightly bemused by this rather strange singer. This was especially apparent when he questioned her about the internet rumours that she may have been born with male genitalia, to which she replied, 'I have a donkey dick!'

But it wasn't her supposed schlong that was making the headlines, it was her purple china cup, which she was spotted with again and again during her stay. In fact, the heat around the cup became so intense that it was generating stories all by itself. One night, as she headed out to dinner at the Metropolitan, Gaga realized she had left the cup back at her suite at Blake's Hotel. Not wanting to be apart from it, she frantically sent a taxi to pick it up and bring it back to her. Acres of column inches followed and her spokespeople seemingly enjoyed the fuss created, batting off media questions with a curt: 'Lady Gaga does not want to reveal anything about the cup itself, but drinking ginger tea is good for singers.'

It became clear that Lady Gaga was enjoying the cup's press coverage and that she was poking fun at the media. 'My teacup is so famous,' she was reported to have said. 'I yelled at her today and I said, "You're stealing my thunder, go to bed!"' She later explained that the cup did have a personal meaning for her: 'I used to have tea at home every day with my mother.' She added that she preferred to drink out of a china cup because she thought it was wasteful to drink out of a paper cup. So she was both environmentally conscious and sentimental! Whether any of this was true remains uncertain, but more than likely this was part of her performance art. And the press and her fans were reacting to it in just the way she wanted them to.

Her whirlwind visit to the UK may have left the fans gasping for air as they attempted to keep up with her strange behaviour, but when she landed on Russian soil, she managed to bewilder even more people. During a press conference Gaga casually revealed that she liked pornography and gays, and let slip that her grandmother liked to check out her legs when she danced, which ruffled a few conservative feathers. Later, when she took to the stage, she told everyone that she loved money, and suggested that they all get drunk that night then go home and have sex. But the next day during a fashion shoot in Red Square, for which she was dressed in a leather leotard, Moscow's authorities decided enough was enough and promptly swooped on her. 'The police came out of nowhere,' she later told the *Sun*. 'They clapped their fingers, which I think means "whore" in Russian.'

When she returned to her home country things took a more domestic turn, as her ex, Speedy, got back in touch. The pair swiftly reunited but their relationship remained volatile. When Gaga caused a scene in a grocery store in a see-through catsuit he reportedly got upset with her and told her off. It seemed clear that things were still far from perfect between them.

Away from her personal life, Gaga continued on her Fame Ball Tour and played to a star-studded audience at trendy New York venue Terminal 5. The likes of Cyndi Lauper and fashionistas such as Zac Posen packed into the VIP areas to catch a glimpse of the most talked-about woman in the world. More excitingly, the previously most-talked about woman – Madonna – was also in attendance with her daughter Lourdes and then-boyfriend Jesus Luz. Gaga was of course excited to have a star of such stature watching her, especially as she had adored her so much as she grew up. 'I was very humbled that Madonna came to the show,' she gushed to MTV. 'I had been hearing all week that she was going to come and I was like "Oh, OK," and I didn't want to talk about it or tell anyone because I thought it was kind of likely that she wouldn't want to come at all.' She added, 'She didn't have to come; she knows that when she shows up it affects the way people perceive me. I always think people that are like that are real class acts.'

After her US leg of the tour, Gaga caught up with The Pussycat Dolls in Australia, where she received a very warm reception. However, the press were keen to find trouble between her and the burlesque group, suggesting that the girls might be growing increasingly unhappy about her outrageous persona and the fact they she was beginning to steal their spotlight. The band and Gaga both played down the rumours, but the press ran with the story that there was some kind of bitter rivalry. *The Age* stoked the flames by describing Gaga's opening set as 'part marketing genius, part art project' that made the Dolls all the more disappointing when they hit the stage. The Melbourne paper sniped: 'At least they can say they once supported the great Lady Gaga.'

Once the Aussie leg was completed and Gaga dealt with the news that her 'Paparazzi' video had been leaked online ahead of its official release (she would ask Perez Hilton to premiere the video on his blog), she decided to head off to Hawaii for a romantic getaway with Speedy.

Since she had hit the big time, Gaga was adamant that she wanted to keep her private life away from the press, especially when it came to matters of the heart. So when she and Speedy arrived in Honolulu, she was determined that the couple's precious time remained intimate and private. But that didn't stop the paps with their long lenses from snapping them as they lounged in the sun. Unfortunately, there was nothing she could do about this less welcome aspect of global fame.

In any case, relaxing breaks and Gaga were not good bedfellows, and her schedule remained jam-packed. No sooner had she washed off her suntan lotion than she was on the move again. After finishing her tour in Asia, she headed to Canada for the Much Music Awards in Toronto where she won Best International Video for 'Poker Face'. Then she was off to Europe again to continue on her Fame Ball Tour and play some big European festivals, including Glastonbury. While she was in the UK she was lined up to support Take That on their reunion tour, which would introduce her to an even wider fanbase of young girls and women over a certain age.

Though her support slot was a piece of cake, her plans for Glastonbury proved more challenging. Unlike her previous appearances, this was her first time performing with a live band – after all, this was a rock festival, so it seemed only right for her to have a proper band backing her. She needn't have worried: her performance went down a storm with the fussy Glastonbury crowd, who were more used to grungy rockers with screeching guitars. Instead, they witnessed a pop goddess gyrating across the stage in a series of oddball outfits. After singing 'Boys Boys Boys', Gaga looked out to the crowd and shouted: 'How are you, my Little Monsters? Are you having a good time?' The wild reaction she received only reassured her that they had enjoyed every single moment of her intricately crafted show. But in spite of the great crowd reaction, what was most talked about after the festival wasn't her staging or her costumes or her songs – it was what was supposedly spotted dangling between her legs beneath her dress.

Just before she launched into her song 'Money Honey', Gaga, by now clad in a figure-hugging red dress, climbed off a motorcycle onstage and then went to pull down her dress. As she did so, eagle-eyed viewers of the telecast on BBC3 noticed what looked like a male member. Although she didn't bring attention to the supposed appendage, it didn't stop fans reopening the internet debate which had been raging for a while about whether or not this 'lady' was actually a hermaphrodite.

The rumours were helped in part by Gaga's own apparent

admission in a blog that she was blessed with both male and female sex organs: 'It's not something that I'm ashamed of, it just isn't something that I go around telling everyone,' she was reported to have said. 'Yes. I have both male and female genitalia, but I consider myself a female. It's just a little bit of a penis and really doesn't interfere much with my life. The reason I haven't talked about it is that it's not a big deal to me. Like, come on. It's not like we all go around talking about our vags. I think this is a great opportunity to make other multiple-gendered people feel more comfortable with their bodies. I'm sexy, I'm hot. I have both a poon and a peener. Big f*cking deal.' Why Gaga chose to say this in the first place – assuming she really did – is questionable, but unsurprisingly, the reaction was what Gaga would have wanted. The mystique surrounding her was merely reinforced and people were left scratching their heads as to what to make of her.

She herself was preoccupied with more serious news, however, having learned of the sudden death of Michael Jackson, who had been found unconscious at his LA home on 25 June 2009. It would later emerge that she was to have performed with him during his upcoming This Is It residency at London's O2 Arena, which he had launched just weeks before. According to press reports, Gaga had been so upset she locked herself away in her dressing room. She was so grief-stricken that she was forced to pull out of a show with Take That at Old Trafford, which supposedly angered lead singer Gary Barlow because she decided to do so only after she had sound-checked. Nevertheless, all was forgiven when she returned a few days later for Take That's barnstorming show at Wembley. She may have missed her chance to perform with the King of Pop, but Gaga was fast becoming pop royalty herself.

Chapter 21:
The Androgyny Strain

Although her songs were catchy enough to become massive hits, what made Gaga stand out from the crowd was her kooky style. And as time went on, and her fame increased, she felt the need to push the envelope even further by wearing garments that beggared belief. At an MTV press conference in Malta she emerged wearing a black mask over her face; in Denmark she wore what looked like a huge purple beehive; while after a gig in Hamburg she turned up to a bar in just lingerie. Gaga had pledged that she would live the life of a pop star for her fans and that they'd never see her in anything ordinary. And it looked like she was holding up her end of the bargain. When she played the Scottish festival T in the Park in 2009, she dazzled in a sculptural mirrorball dress and face mask, but surely her most outrageous outfit up to this point was the one she wore for a TV interview in Germany – a coat made out of dozens of Kermit frogs, designed by Jean-Charles de Castelbajac and topped with a Kermit fascinator. While most people were stunned by the garment, Gaga explained that the coat had a meaning. 'I thought it was a commentary on not wearing fur, because I hate fur and I don't wear fur,' she told Ryan Seacrest when he quizzed her about her outfit.

Gaga later explained that her clothes always had some kind of relevance. She didn't merely throw on a dress just because it looked nice. Her outfits were the results of a thought process that gave them context and meaning. 'Everything you see me do is in some way inspired by these visions in my brain that happen because of the way I live my life,' she told reporters during her stay at the T in the Park festival. 'Every time you see me, it's performance. When I'm sleeping, it's performance.'

Gaga admitted that unlike other female stars, her particular brand of fashion was not to project an image of sexiness. On the contrary, it was a way of expressing herself. 'I look like such a tranny,' she laughed to *Fab* mag when asked how she feels when she looks at pictures of herself. 'I look like Grace Jones, androgynous, robo, future fashion queen. It's not what is sexy. It's graphic, it's art. Yeah, I take my pants off but does it matter if your pants are off if you've got eight-inch shoulder pads on and a hood and black lipstick and glasses with rocks on them? I don't know. That's sexy to me. But I don't think anybody's d*** is hard looking at that! I think they're confused and maybe a little scared.'

Whether that was true or not, her avant-garde garb was definitely making an impact on her fellow celebs. Rihanna, Katy Perry, Lily Allen – to name a few – were spotted out in some very peculiar outfits indeed. Rihanna shamelessly attended an Independence Day bash with silver sequins stuck to her nipples, while a few days later she was seen wearing black duct tape across them, a look Gaga had sported several months before.

Meanwhile, Gaga's relationship with Speedy hit the rocks again when the *Sun* newspaper printed pictures of her supposedly smooching a chap at Balans in London's Soho. According to reports, a jealous Speedy decided enough was enough and called time on the relationship once and for all. Gaga admitted she wasn't the settling-down type. 'Part of me would love [marriage], but the bigger part of me knows it's never going to happen,' she told *Music News*. 'I don't think I'm cut out for love and marriage. Music and my art are the big things in my life. I know whatever happens they won't cheat on me and they'll never let me down. Men nearly always do.'

While this may have been true, like any girl she didn't relish the break-up of a relationship. But she was also a tough cookie and was quite able to live her life without a relationship. She was independent and proud. 'I don't need a man,' she told the *Sun*. 'I might sometimes want a man, but I don't need one. I earn my money, I create my art, I know where I am going. I think my parents thought I'd be married by now. But I rebelled against that my whole life. I'm unconventional, I'm a rebel.'

But while her love life was nothing to write home about, her career was still going from strength to strength. Not only were 'Poker Face' and 'Just Dance' in the top ten of the top fifty digital songs of all time, 'LoveGame' had notched up 18 million views on YouTube and was also a chart topper, which meant she was one of only three artists in America to have three number 1 singles off a debut album. Not only that, Gaga was also nominated in nine categories at the MTV Awards, including Best New Artist, Best Female Video, Video of the Year and Best Pop Video for 'Poker Face'.

The Fame Ball Tour continued, stopping off in Asia where she had a tattoo of a quote from German poet Rainer Maria Rilke which read: 'In the deepest hour of the night, confess to yourself that you would die if you were forbidden to write. And look deep into your heart where it spreads its roots, the answer, and ask yourself, must I write?'

Gaga was very taken with the poet, admitting: 'I love Rilke. It's no secret I live my life almost in utter submission and loyalty to Rilke. It's important to be objective about your own work and what I've learnt through my love of Warhol is to empower the people around you to feed your creativity. Criticism can be wonderful if you have a strong sense of what you're creating. If you have an incessant need for validation from an outside place that is not yourself – that is when criticism can be not just detrimental but life-changing to your work.'

Back in the UK for the V festival, Gaga caused a minor storm. Not only did she demand in her rider that organizers have a purple cup of English tea ready for her at all times, she also failed to make it onstage punctually, which left her Little Monsters very unhappy indeed. In fact, the longer the impatient throng waited the more angry they became, resulting in many of them booing and trying to start a slow handclap. Finally Gaga emerged triumphantly and put on what she would describe as an 'incredible' show. However, due to her lateness, organizers cut her appearance short, which left the crowd baying for blood once again. Never one to let her fans down, Gaga begged them to forgive her: 'My fans were lovely and really deserved to hear "Poker Face". I love you and I'm sorry,' she tweeted, adding in a statement: 'Stage manager pulled the plug because I was five minutes over my time at V Fest! Show was incredible. A shame people have no respect for music.'

Meanwhile in the press, Gaga apparently came under attack from both Róisín Murphy, who had a hit with 'Sing It Back', who claimed in the *Daily Mail* that Gaga had copied her style (she would later deny she ever said this), and Tori Amos, who dismissed her as a 'meteor star' – a singer who entertained only for a while (*Evening Herald*, Ireland). As with her run-in with Christina Aguilera, Gaga kept a dignified silence and continued on her way – no doubt amused that these high-profile rival stars were merely keeping her in the headlines.

However, speaking to SHOWstudio.com a while later, she admitted that her fashion inspirations were in fact Brit fashionistas Daphne Guinness and Isabella Blow. 'Isabella and Daphne are two genius human beings – women, icons – but so much more than that. They are for me a way to look into myself and examine their lives and who they are in an effort to understand myself better. Isabella is an enormous inspiration and so is Daphne, I cherish their lives – the late Isabella and the living, breathing and beautiful Daphne, whom I could not live without . . . It's very funny just to say that before I met Daphne, I used to get confused for her all the time. People would say: "Daphne!" or they'd say: "Do you know Daphne? She will love you." "My God, you look like Isabella." I would terrify people, particularly Philip [Treacy, the milliner] and Lee [Alexander McQueen]. The same for Daphne, people have said: "I love your music!" and she's like, "I'm not Gaga!" . . . She's a creature, a beautiful creature.'

Yet despite the waves she was making in the fashion world, it was the gay scene where she continued to feel most at home, even though she was worried it might appear she was trying to exploit the gay market. Her gay fans had been among the first group of people to embrace her and her music, in the same way fans of Madonna and Kylie had done years before. But as the press started to focus further on this aspect of her appeal, she became concerned that she was becoming one of those artists who were using sexuality to sell records. 'I'm very careful about the way I write about sexuality,' she said in *Fab* magazine. 'I push the boundaries in everything I do, I have a lot of girl-on-girl in my short films and there's a lot of boy-on-boy onstage. I'm not trying to use my gay fans to get a fan base; I really genuinely love them and that's why I made the decision early on not to play "Boys Boys Boys" in the clubs right away. I didn't want to be seen like I was trying to promote a song that was like a gay club anthem.'

In fact, she said she wanted *all* her songs to be gay anthems, songs that would touch the hearts of her gay fans. She was adamant that she didn't want people to think she was being deliberately controversial by touching on gay sensibilities, as some artists had. 'Anybody that writes music that touches on sexuality or gay anything is setting themselves up to be a target for questioning and interrogation, but I appreciate when people ask me those questions so I can tell it how it is,' she said. (*Fab* magazine)

But her fans knew where she stood. 'The real motivation is to just turn the world gay,' she told an interviewer from *OUT* magazine. 'I very much want to inject gay culture into the mainstream. I committed myself to them and they committed themselves to me and because of the gay community I'm where I am today. I feel intrinsically inclined toward a more gay lifestyle. I myself am not a gay woman, I am a free-spirited woman. I have had boyfriends and I have hooked up with women, but it's never been like, "I've discovered gayness when I was dot dot dot."'

Despite her trying to play her sexuality down, the press continued to focus on the subject and rehash the rumours that she was a hermaphrodite. At first Gaga found the whole fascination about her nether regions highly amusing, joking about it on chat shows and at her gigs, but after a while the joke started to wear thin. When she was asked about the ongoing rumours during an interview the *Matt and Jo Show* in Australia, she lost her rag. 'It's too lowbrow to even discuss,' she snapped. 'I've made fun of it before but to talk about it is ridiculous. I'm an accomplished musician and I'd rather talk about my fans and my music.' When she appeared at a press conference in Germany, where she was launching her Heartbeats headphones, she snapped at a TV personality called Collien Fernandes who had asked her if she had a penis: 'My vagina is offended by this question.' Fernandes was then removed from the press conference.

In spite of her growing irritation with the speculation about whether or not she was a man or a woman, Gaga did admit that she could understand why there was this fascination with her genitalia. 'It's society's reaction to a strong woman,' she told MTV News. 'The idea that we equate strength with men and a penis is a symbol of male strength, it's just what it is. But like I said, I'm not offended, but my vagina is a little upset!'

Chapter 22:
Healing a Broken Heart

Her vagina – or lack of one – may have been the subject on everyone's lips, but Gaga didn't have time to waste thinking about what other people thought about her genitals. She had the huge MTV Awards ceremony to look forward to and with nine nominations, she wanted to make sure that whether or not she would walk away with a gong she would at least put on a show that viewers would never forget.

Meanwhile, more good news arrived. 'Poker Face' was named the most downloaded song ever in both the US and the UK, with 'Just Dance' the third most downloaded in this country. It was an extraordinary achievement, and set her up for a showstopping appearance at the MTV Awards.

When the awards night finally arrived, Gaga knew that she had to make a big impression. And with her sense of style and wicked sense of humour, she did just that. Even though she was dressed in a typically ridiculous outfit – a Victorian-style high necked dress with feathers, a golden mask straight out of *The Phantom of the Opera* and a golden neck brace – what got the paps going wild was that the date in her limousine was none other than TV legend and sex god Kermit the frog! 'He's been a really good date,' she told MTV.

'It's our first date but we've been eyeing each other for a while.' As she strolled into the auditorium, she couldn't help but think back to the days when she was a kid, pretending that she was striding down the red carpet at the MTV Awards. And here she was, years later, doing just that.

Throughout the show, Gaga changed her clothes so many times that those packed into the ceremony at New York's Radio City Music Hall could barely keep up. To accept her Best New Artist award she donned a striking red lace outfit, including a mask covering her entire face. She removed the mask to give thanks to 'God and her gays', while later, when Beyoncé won Video of the Year, the camera focused on Gaga who was now wearing what looked like a white wreath-type head wrap.

But her costume changes were nothing compared to her controversial stage performance of 'Paparazzi', which saw her dripping blood and hanging on a rope.

The performance began with Gaga lying on the floor, her face hidden behind a beaded mask with feather horns, being helped to her feet by a gaggle of male dancers. Wearing white knee-high boots and a belly-baring unitard with a single feathered shoulder pad, she began to sing a few lines of 'Poker Face' before launching into 'Paparazzi'. Staggering around the stage with a cane, Gaga pirouetted behind a dancer in a lily-white wheelchair before sitting at a white grand piano, where she rested one foot on the keyboard as she played it. Then, as she stumbled away from the piano, blood began to trickle down her midriff while she sang about media vultures. Her dancers piled in around her as she collapsed, before being hoisted up on a rope looking very dead indeed while the sound of camera shutters sounded out and a golden halo was projected on the big screen behind her.

Unsurprisingly, the crowd of seasoned performers, which included her idol Madonna, was left in stunned silence as they took in the performance art they had just seen. This was more than just a stage routine for a music show – Gaga had created a theatre piece that went far beyond merely visualizing a song. She told *Rolling Stone* afterwards: 'I just wanted to say something honest and real and not just give a performance where I was just jacking off onstage the whole time about my record. It was really for my fans who I knew would be at home cheering and swooning.'

With the awards now out of the way, Gaga looked forward to her upcoming Fame Kills Tour, which she would co-headline with Kanye West, an idea that had been mooted some time before the MTV Awards. However, after his strange behaviour at the awards – during which he drunkenly jumped up onstage as Taylor Swift accepted her Best Video gong and told her that Beyoncé had deserved it instead – rumours began to circulate that the tour might be cancelled. Despite the fact Kanye appeared on countless TV shows afterwards apologizing for his actions, it was later confirmed that the Fame Kills Tour would not go ahead. Gaga told *Rolling Stone*: 'It just wasn't the right timing, to go on tour with Kanye. I don't want to embellish on it too much because I want to respect Kanye's privacy but we just had our own reasons. We're real friends, real friends make decisions like that . . . But who's to say what will happen in the future?'

Obviously disappointed by the news, Gaga was able to find solace in the fact that 'Just Dance' had won Best Video Award at the *Q* Awards in London and that she had been named 2009's Up and Coming Woman at *Billboard* magazine's annual Woman of the Year awards, adding to her growing collection of music-business honours.

It was around this time that Gaga and Madonna fans' dreams came true when they both agreed to appear on *Saturday Night Live* together. This was perhaps rather unexpected: since Gaga had burst on to the scene, some critics had lazily described her as a Madonna copycat, and the press was eager to whip up an imagined feud between them. However, neither star had been pulled into the argument, with Madonna even telling reporters that she was very flattered that people were comparing her to someone as influential and well-received as Gaga. On the show they enjoyed taking at pop at those who thought they were at loggerheads. Both dressed in skimpy black outfits, they stepped out onstage to sing a duet, spitting barbs like, 'What's wrong, Madonna, can't get into the groove?' – to which Madonna replies, 'What the hell is a disco stick?' adding 'What kind of name is Lady Gaga? It sounds like baby food.' Eventually the feisty pair end up catfighting onstage, pulling at each other's hair. Needless to say, the hilarious skit went down a storm.

But Madonna wasn't the only star Gaga collaborated with in October 2009. Beyoncé also got in touch with her to ask her to join her on her song 'Video Phone'. The result was a jagged R&B tune coupled with a video in which Gaga had never looked so normal, pulling off something of a Golden Era Hollywood look, complete with exquisite make-up and luscious blonde locks cascading across her perfect shoulders.

At this point in her career, Gaga was on a high. Her records were selling like hot cakes, her fans were more devoted than ever and she was gaining the respect she deserved from the critics. But little did she know that her life was about to take a dark turn. First of all, she was left devastated when she found out that her Great Dane Rumpus had died suddenly, aged five. The dog's death was devastating to the star, for he and his mother were very much part of the Haus of Gaga family. If that wasn't bad enough, shortly afterwards, when Gaga strolled up the red carpet at the Ace Music Awards, dressed in a black veiled outfit, a photographer collapsed in front of her and died upon arriving at hospital. Although she didn't know the pap, watching him collapse before her was profoundly disturbing.

But the worst was yet to come, when news reached her that her father Joseph had been rushed to hospital suffering from chest pains. Once admitted, he was told that he would have to undergo surgery, which a worried Gaga insisted on paying for. 'I haven't bought anything yet with the money I have made from my record,' she told her father. 'Let me buy you a new heart!'

The operation was a devastating prospect for Gaga. To have her father, who had inspired her for so many years, sick in a hospital bed terrified her more than anything else. Keeping her fans up to date with Joseph's condition, she tweeted: 'My daddy had open-heart surgery today. And after long hours, and lots of tears, they healed his broken heart, and mine. Speechless.' Later she updated her Twitter feed with the touching information: 'At the hospital. Giving Daddy a foot rub while he falls asleep. He's my hero!'

She later revealed that the whole episode was 'the biggest nightmare in my life. My father is my whole world; I'm such a daddy's girl.'

She told *Elle* magazine the day after his surgery: 'I just wanted to have him walk me down the aisle and hold my babies. I mean, not tomorrow! But in eight to ten years, I want to have babies for my dad to hold, grandkids. And I want to have a husband who loves and supports me, just the way anyone else does.'

While her father was in recovery, Gaga, her sister and mother took turns by his bedside. Too worried to leave the hospital, she spent days without having a shower. According to *Vanity Fair*, one day while she was sitting by him, caressing his hand in hers, her father leaned over and said to her, 'Hey, kid, you know, you got a reputation to uphold. Why don't you go home, take a shower, brush your hair, and put some make-up on? I know it'll make you feel better.' Taking her father's advice, she went home and put some lipstick on before returning. And he said, 'There she is, there's my girl.' Her father knew that even in the darkest of times, Gaga needed to shine.

Chapter 23:
The Fame Monster

Once she knew her father was on the road to recovery, Gaga focused her mind on the reissued version of her album *The Fame*, entitled *The Fame Monster*. While it featured the songs from the original album, she had written and recorded a handful of new tracks while touring the world, eight of which were also included.

Speaking to the *Daily Star* about the new title, she explained: 'I have an obsession with death and sex. Those two things are also the nexus of horror films, which I've been obsessing over lately. I've been watching horror movies and 1950s science fiction movies. My re-release is called *The Fame Monster* so I've just been sort of bulimically eating and regurgitating monster movies and all things scary. I've just been noticing a resurgence of this idea of monster, of fantasy, but in a very real way.' She added, 'If you notice in those films, there's always a juxtaposition of sex with death. That's what makes it so scary. Body and mind are primed for orgasm and instead somebody gets killed.'

Gaga further explained the content matter of *The Fame Monster* to the *Daily Star*. 'I'm kind of obsessing over the decay of the celebrity and the way that fame is a monster in society. That's what my new record is about, so it was kind of a perfect fit.' She continued,

'While travelling the world for two years, I've encountered several monsters, each represented by a different song on the new record: my "Fear of Sex Monster", my "Fear of Alcohol Monster", my "Fear of Love Monster", my "Fear of Death Monster", my "Fear of Loneliness Monster", etc. I spent a lot of nights in Eastern Europe, and this album is a pop experimentation with industrial/Goth beats, nineties dance melodies, an obsession with the lyrical genius of eighties melancholic pop, and the runway [catwalk].'

The cover artwork for the album was shot by Hedi Slimane and sees Gaga looking like a Space Age geisha on the Deluxe version and a grungier-looking Gaga with straggly dark hair on the main version. It transpired her record label was concerned that fans would be put off by the latter image because it didn't look pop enough.

'My record label didn't want to put out that photo that's my album cover, with the brown hair,' she told *Rolling Stone*. 'They were like, "It's confusing, it's too dark, you look gothic, it's not pop," and I said, "You don't know what pop is, because everyone was telling me I wasn't pop last year, and now look – so don't tell me what pop is, I know what pop is." It's funny, because I fought and fought and fought, and I actually ended up having two covers, because I wanted to do this yin and yang presentation with the covers. When I go to see what my fans are saying, I go on to GagaDaily – they see the cover and say, "I don't really like the blonde one, but the brown one is f★★★ing sick." They love it, and I know what they love, so I make it for them, I don't care what anybody else wants.'

The lead single was 'Bad Romance', a ferociously energetic pop song with a dark lyric, which was produced by RedOne in Amsterdam. He also co-produced 'Alejandro' and 'Monster' (which she says was written about being in love with a bad boy whom she keeps going back to). Her favourite song on the album was 'Speechless', a ballad that she wrote about the fear of losing her father. Speaking about how the song came about, she revealed:

'My mom called me and I was very depressed,' she said. 'I was on tour and I couldn't leave so I went into the studio and I wrote this song "Speechless" and it's about these phone calls. My dad used to call me after he'd had a few drinks and I wouldn't know what to say. I was speechless and I just feared that I would lose him and I wouldn't be there.'

Also featured on the album was a sassy tune called 'Telephone', which was originally written with Britney Spears in mind, and recorded with Beyoncé.

'Bad Romance' was debuted at her friend Alexander McQueen's Spring/Summer 2010 Paris Fashion Week as a soundtrack to his show. It was also later used in the 'Last Days of Disco' episode of *Gossip Girl*, in which Gaga played a small cameo as herself at the school prom. In its first week of release in the US it entered the *Billboard* Hot 100 at number 9, and would become her fifth chart-topper.

The video was equally popular online, with fans desperate to see Gaga's latest creative offering. Directed by Francis Lawrence, who had dreamt up promos for Destiny's Child, Britney Spears and Janet Jackson as well as directing the movie *I Am Legend*, the video features Gaga being kidnapped by a group of supermodels who dope her and try to sell her off to the Russian Mafia as a sex slave. Gaga said she enjoyed working with Lawrence because there was 'a meeting of minds'.

With the reworked album in the shops, Gaga was intent on taking it on the road. The show was, as expected, a sensation. Opening with the eighties discofest that is 'Dance In The Dark', the show was a visual blur of wild outfits and crazier choreography. Her fans – or her Little Monsters as she was now calling them – lapped it all up, even if the press were scandalized by Gaga's sexual behaviour onstage. At one point, her breasts were groped by her dancers, while during another segment a dancer carried her across the stage by the crotch – shocking to the press, but nothing the fans hadn't seen before.

After the show Gaga thanked her Haus of Gaga team, explaining: 'It's a real bond and relationship and that's what I think music and art is about. They are my heart and soul. They believe in me and they look at me like a mother and daughter and sister, with pride and love.'

As 2009 came to an end, she was in the UK again, performing 'Bad Romance' on *The X Factor* in a big bath surrounded by her dancers. According to reports at the time, Gaga was ordered by the show's producers to bear in mind the series' youthful audience and keep her performance tasteful, which she did. After the show she was spotted in the Devonshire Arms, a pub in Acton, west London, where, dressed in a miniskirt, grey blazer and black military hat, she ate fish and chips in the lounge bar. Manager David Haberlin said: 'She came in about 7.15 p.m. She just wanted to have a traditional British meal and she had our fish and chips. Then she was happy to sign a few autographs and have her picture taken. Afterwards she said she had enjoyed herself and said thanks for the meal. She was very polite and well-mannered.' This was the second time she had enjoyed pub grub. A few days before she had been spotted lounging in a booth in a Blackpool bar between rehearsals for the Royal Variety Performance, where she was to sing her gorgeous ballad 'Speechless' in front of the Queen.

Gaga arrived onstage to close the annual show with a twenty-foot train trailing behind her Elizabeth I-inspired red PVC dress. She was then helped on to a chair attached to a chain and hoisted thirty feet in the air to play a piano which was supported by legs like those of the giant elephants in the Salvador Dali painting, *The Temptation of St Anthony*.

After the lavish show, still dressed in her regal PVC finery, Gaga met Her Majesty backstage, who told her that she had enjoyed her stunning performance. It was a fitting end to what had been a memorable year.

★

The start of 2010 saw Gaga continue on her Monster Ball Tour around the globe and doing her charitable part by donating proceeds from some of her shows to the relief campaign for Haiti, which had been rocked by a catastrophic earthquake. But as she drifted from date to date, she decided that the show needed freshening up. 'I'm throwing out the stage,' she revealed in *Rolling Stone*. 'My team thinks I am completely psychotic. But I don't f★★★ing care what they think.' Her idea was to increase the size of the staging to four times that of the existing show. The costumes were given a revamp, as were the set pieces. The show was also given a New York theme and told a story in which Gaga and her pals are lost in the city and are looking for the Monster Ball. Fans, unsurprisingly, loved the new additions.

Meanwhile, away from music, Gaga was invited to team up with Cyndi Lauper to become the new spokeswomen for the MAC Viva Glam campaign, which raises money through cosmetic sales for HIV/AIDS programmes. She threw herself into the role wholeheartedly. 'I have been a huge, huge fan of MAC since I was very young. MAC is a lifestyle, this mecca near my house where I knew I could be whoever I wanted to be and really find myself as an individual and feel confident and secure, ' she told CNN. She went on to speak passionately about the need for women to get tested for HIV, and to say that she and Cyndi were determined to remind the world that AIDS was not just a gay disease, but one that also affected all women.

'I think that that's the very sort of pre-assumption that is the reason that women aren't getting tested and the reason that women are allowing the negotiations to go on in the bedroom and not really putting their foot down. And, you know, these lipsticks, don't just give them to your single friends, give them to your taken friends and to your taken mother as a reminder to protect their own life, because we see every day people are in committed relationships for years that are betrayed and people are disloyal. And it's very important to at least remind yourself to get tested, and your partner, as well.'

Gaga was certainly throwing herself into her charity work, and, coupled with her heavy workload, it was soon reported that friends feared she was on the verge of collapsing. But while her pals may have been concerned, Gaga seemed to be happy with her lot. 'I don't go to nightclubs,' she admitted to *Rolling Stone*. 'If I do I'll be one whisky and a half into it and then I have to get back to work. I love my work so much, I find it really hard to go out and have a good time.'

One downside to her fame was the fact that being constantly on tour meant that she rarely got to see her friends. When she was asked about the low points that came with her career, she told the Mebourne-based *Herald Sun*: 'Loneliness, being on the road. I have a chronic sadness that recurs. The lowest point was in Australia. I was overwhelmingly sad and I didn't know why because I had all these things to be happy about. I went to the studio and played for hours and I wrote what is going to be the greatest record of my career, a beautiful song about my father ['Speechless']. I remember watching the mascara tears flood the ivories and I thought, "It's OK to be sad!"'

But loneliness wasn't the only fallout from her constant touring. It started to affect her health, too, and she found herself having to cancel a gig at Indiana's Purdue University after she fainted. Never normally one to cancel a show, she tweeted: 'I have been crying for hours, I feel like I let my fans down tonight.' She went on to explain that an hour before the show she had felt dizzy and had trouble breathing. When paramedics arrived they told her that she had an irregular heartbeat which they thought was the result of exhaustion and dehydration. 'Everyone was concerned I would be in danger during the two-hour show,' she said. 'I am so devastated. I have performed with the flu, with strep throat. I would never cancel a show just based on discomfort.'

Once she was better, she joined Elton John at the Grammys to perform a duet of his classic 'Your Song' and her tender ballad 'Speechless'. The performance started with the curtain rising to reveal a flamboyant stage set with the words 'The Fame Factory' hanging above the stage. A master of ceremonies stepped through the dancers, shouting, 'The real Gaga comes complete with five number 1 singles . . . and she has no soul!' Behind him Gaga appeared in a cage and began to sing a cabaret version of 'Poker Face', before launching into the more traditional version. One of her dancers then dragged her offstage and dumped her in a 'rejected' bin. Moments later she re-emerged, covered in ash sitting at a huge piano with two keyboards for her duet with Elton John, who was also daubed in ash. The performance was a showstopper and when it ended the guests in the auditorium gave them a standing ovation.

And the night just kept getting better. Nominated for five Grammys, she eventually came away with two – Best Dance Recording for 'Poker Face' and Best Dance Album for *The Fame*.

It seemed the world couldn't be a better place for Gaga at this point. But just as her career was soaring into the heavens, she was rocked by a tragedy that left her devastated. News emerged that her close friend, the world-famous designer Alexander McQueen, had been found dead in his London flat. It appeared he had taken his own life. Gaga had worked closely with the designer over the past year or so, in particular on the video for 'Bad Romance', in which she could be seen strutting around in a pair of McQueen's infamous lobster–claw heels and runway designs. She even showed up to many high-profile events in his wild garments, including the red lace see-through outfit she wore when she accepted the award for Best New Artist during the 2009 MTV VMAs. Their relationship had become so strong that McQueen's publicist had referred to Gaga as 'an unofficial muse'.

At the Brit Awards a couple of weeks later, a still-upset Gaga performed two songs – 'Telephone' and 'Brown Eyes' – which she dedicated to McQueen. Fans online were disappointed by the lacklustre songs, and pop critic Paul Morley described her performance as 'epic and silly, hyper and banal, expensive and tacky, self-important narcissistic nonsense'. But despite her sombre mood, Gaga took away the three Brit Awards she was nominated for: Best International Female, International Breakthrough Act and Best International Album.

Shortly afterwards, Gaga released the single 'Telephone', which came complete with a ten-minute video directed by Jonas Åkerlund. Inspired by Tarantino's *Kill Bill*, it sees Gaga bailed out of jail by Beyoncé before the two of them go on a killing spree. The video, shot in just two days, was a visual treat to the eye – colourful, stylish, funny and dramatic. It was almost like a mini-movie – which was the effect Åkerlund was after. 'We usually don't do opening credits for videos, but it kind of goes with the story and the length of the video,' he told MTV. He also explained that Gaga had asked to use the real car from *Kill Bill*, which Tarantino had sanctioned. 'We were gonna have a convertible hearse, but then Gaga had some sort of meeting with Quentin [Tarantino] and he offered to lend his car. We thought that was fun too.'

Also joining her in her video were her pals Semi Precious Weapons and singer Tyrese Gibson. But while the plot of the video was gripping enough, it was the dance routines featuring Gaga and Beyoncé that caught the eye. 'It's just like the big dance number with Beyoncé in it,' Jonas explained. 'This is how professional she is – she actually rehearsed on the day Gaga and her dancers had rehearsed a little bit before and pretty much nailed it.'

As the track topped the charts across the world, Gaga became something of a talking point yet again. But although *Time* magazine was busy claiming she was one of the most influential people on the planet, one notable voice rang out in dissent. Gaga's idol Grace Jones, whom she had met not so long before and described the experience as 'amazing', took a swipe at the global sensation. When asked about

Gaga, Grace reportedly told the *Guardian*: 'I really don't think of her at all. I go about my business.' When pushed on whether or not she thought Gaga had been heavily influenced by her, she snapped: 'Well, you know, I've seen some things she's worn that I've worn, and that does kind of p*** me off.' She also let slip that Gaga had been in touch with her to discuss the possibility of a duet between the two of them. But she told the *Guardian* that she wasn't interested because 'I'd just prefer to work with someone who is more original and someone who is not copying me, actually.' Ouch! For any other singer this might have come as a devastating setback, but for Gaga it was just a minor blip in a continuing wave of success. And in any case, now she was ready to have her own say . . .

Chapter 24:
Gaga Speaks (and Speaks)

Never one to shy away from the press, Gaga seemed to spend much of the spring and summer of 2010 looking out at her fans from magazine covers as she promoted the release of 'Alejandro', which some critics dubbed her 'La Isla Bonita'. Again the song went down a storm, although some religious groups like the Catholic League found elements of the video blasphemous, in particular the segment in which Gaga swallows a set of rosary beads. The fashion photographer Steven Klein, who had directed the video, dismissed the scene as Gaga's 'desire to take in the holy'.

To coincide with the release, British music monthly *Q* hit newsstands in the UK featuring a topless Gaga on the cover boasting what looked very much like a penis bulge. The shoot had taken place some four months before when she had been in the UK, but it would later emerge it had not gone smoothly. It was Gaga who had initially approached the editors of *Q* with an idea too good to resist. She told them she wanted to appear naked on the cover with a dildo attached to her. For someone who had recently said her vagina was insulted by all the speculation surrounding her gender, it came as something of a surprise to the *Q* team. But that's what she wanted. 'We all know one of the biggest talking points of the year was that I have a dick,' she said to the magazine's editorial staff. 'So why not give them what they want? I want to comment on it in a beautiful, artistic way. How I wanna show it. And I want to call the piece Lady Gaga Dies Hard!'

After some toing and froing, it was then decided that Gaga wouldn't appear totally naked – she would be partially covered and the dildo would be placed beneath her trousers, creating a bulge. But on the day of the shoot itself, Gaga seemed unhappy and tense. She complained that the lighting wasn't right and that the pictures were not making her look as feminine or as pretty as she wanted. At one point she complained that the lighting accentuated her chin, while at another time she wasn't happy with the light on her face and groin. As the shoot progressed, Gaga apparently became more and more agitated before eventually storming off to her dressing room. After a while she returned behind dark sunglasses, though it was apparent she had been crying. Telling the editorial staff that she wanted to postpone the shoot, she left the set. A month later, Gaga's reps got back in touch with Q and said they'd like to reschedule the shoot on the condition that they could use a photographer of their choice. Q said no and Gaga and her reps never got back in touch again. A planned tour report was subsequently scrapped.

While Q may have ended up offending the biggest pop star on the planet, journalist Caitlin Moran of *The Times* – an ardent Gaga fan – fared somewhat better when she joined her Monster Ball Tour (interview in *The Times*, May 2010). Meeting her backstage in Berlin, Caitlin noted that this tour was like no other she had seen. The walls and ceiling of the star's dressing room were draped in black, making it resemble a 'pop-Gothic seraglio'. Scented candles flickered around the room, a vintage record player rested on the floor surrounded by piles of vinyl, and works of art hung on the walls. And then there was Gaga, just sitting there. 'Two things strike you about her immediately,' Caitlin wrote. 'First, that she really isn't dressed casually. In a breast-length, silver-grey wig, she has a black lace veil wound around her face, and sits, framed, in an immense, custom-made, one-off Alexander McQueen cloak. The effect is one of having been ushered into the presence of a very powerful fairytale queen: possibly one who has recently killed Aslan, on the Stone Table. The second thing you notice is that she is being lovely. Absolutely lovely. Both literally and figuratively; what's under the veil and the cloak is a diminutive, well brought up, New York Catholic girl from a wealthy middle-class family, with twinkly brown eyes and a minxy sense of humour.'

Caitlin went on to detail how Gaga had politely offered her tea in a china cup, and when she teased her about looking so slim, the singer replied curtly, 'But I certainly don't have an eating problem. A little MDMA [Ecstasy] once in a while never killed anybody, but I really don't do drugs. I don't touch cocaine any more. I don't smoke. Well, maybe a single cigarette – with whisky – while I'm working, because it just frees my mind a little bit. But I care about my voice. The thrill of my voice being healthy onstage is really special. I take care of myself.'

When Caitlin quizzed her about the rumours that she was exhausted and how she kept herself sane as the world around went Gaga-mad, she replied flatly: 'Prescription medicine. I can't control my thoughts at all. I'm tortured. But I like that. Lorca says it's good to be tortured. The thoughts are unstoppable – but so is the music. It comes to me constantly.'

However, on the subject of her health, which had been making headlines for the past several months, Gaga did admit that she was concerned about heart palpitations she was suffering from, which she brushed off as fatigue and, mysteriously, 'other things'. She explained how just days earlier, prior to a show in Tokyo, she suffered breathing problems but eventually managed to get out onstage after she was given some oxygen. Gaga hinted that the 'other things' she was referring to might be lupus, the disease that had killed her Aunt Joanne. Lupus is a connective-tissue disease, in which the immune system attacks the body and commonly causes heart palpitations, shortness of breath, joint pain and anaemia, leaving its sufferers exhausted. Although she admitted to Caitlin that she had been tested, she didn't admit to having the condition itself.

Moving away from her supposed illness, Gaga maintained once again that she wasn't in the fame game for money. 'I don't really spend money and I don't really like fame,' she told her. 'You know what I spend most of my money on? Disappearing. I hate the paparazzi. Because the truth is – no matter what people tell you – you can control it. If you put as much money into your security as you put into your cars or your diamonds or your jewellery, you can just . . . disappear. People who say they can't get away are lying. They must just like the . . . big flashes.'

Gaga also took the unusual step of taking a swipe at her fellow stars who moaned about fans who downloaded their material illegally. Surprisingly, she reckoned it was OK for her fans to do so because artists made so much money from touring. 'Big artists can make anywhere from $40 million [£28 million (then)] for one cycle of two years' touring,' she explained. 'Giant artists make upwards of $100 million. Make music – then tour. It's just the way it is today.'

This was not the only revealing interview Gaga gave in the summer of 2010. Speaking to fashion website SHOWstudio.com, she gushed about her Monsters, her devoted brood of fans. 'I feel so blessed,' she said. 'It's so unexplainable, the love I feel for my fans, how they treat me, all the videos they create, the lovely notes and artwork. Just the other day I spent hours reading all this fan mail sent to me, sending back autographs and looking at artwork. I put love into my fans and they put love into me: we continue to give love back forth to each other, forever.' She went on to explain how when she told her fans that her grandfather had been taken ill and admitted to hospital her Twitter feed was filled with kind messages of support with the words 'get well Grandpa Gaga' trending worldwide. 'That', she explained, 'has nothing to do with my music, my clothes or making an album number 1 – that's just pure friendship.'

If that wasn't enough, an emotional Gaga went on to tell SHOWstudio.com how a group of fans had got hold of her number and texted her a picture of themselves dressed up in masks as they headed off to a twenty-first birthday. They told her how inspiring she was to them and that they were wearing the masks because they loved her and because they felt she had changed their lives. Gaga recalled how, when she heard this, she lay in bed crying because she loved them so much. 'I would say most of my fans are quite troubled,' she mused. 'I look into the audience and it's like tiny little mirrors – they remind me of myself. So many of them are insecure, hate their parents, don't fit in at school, are cutters or have depression. Some of them are nine and just like pop music, some are thirty-five and are on a night out with the boys – it varies. I'd say there's a vast majority of them that are troubled, want to fit in and feel like freaks. They want to go out, raise their freak flag high above their head and be freed. My show is a free place for them. I created the show for my fans to have a place to go – a safe place, an electric chapel. It's their hat – their social canopy.'

Many in the industry recognized that Gaga was at the forefront of exploiting new media. The singles downloads had broken records and she had embraced Twitter wholeheartedly, understanding it was a forum where 'you can build trust with your fans – if you use it for the right reasons'. However, she was adamant that she had no time for those Twitter users who used it for their own vanity. 'People that argue on Twitter or are just using it as a celebrity networking device – it's boring and has nothing to do with your fans or your vocational purpose,' she continued. 'I use the internet – I've embraced the internet in a pop cultural kind of way. I think about what a pop artist would have done in the seventies or eighties if the internet was as it is today. Warhol would have done something beyond what I do and what we all do with the internet because it's so powerful and it can reach so many people.'

Gaga also addressed the reasons behind her much-talked-about extreme style and admitted that she rejected the way society is taught to perceive female beauty. 'Women are strong and fragile,' she opined. 'Women are beautiful and ugly. We are soft spoken and loud all at once. There is something mind controlling about the way we're taught to view women.' She went on to argue that her style was a manifestation of her feminist beliefs. 'It's exciting because all of the avant-garde clothing, lyrics and musical style which was, at a certain time, once considered weird, odd, unattractive, uncomfortable, shocking – it's now trendy. Perhaps we can make women's rights trendy. Feminism, strength, security and the power of the wisdom of the woman – let's make that trendy.' (SHOWstudio.com interview)

She went on to broach the subject of Madonna. Since she'd started out, lazy critics had branded her the new millennial Madonna, simply because they shared similar looks, embraced gay culture and were both edgy Italian-American girls who loved their papas. Unsurprisingly, Gaga was only too happy to sing the praises of her pop elder. 'She is so full of the most wonderful freedom and spirit and is so kind,' Gaga said. 'Working with her has always been very exciting and fun: we have shared some wonderful, honest moments together. She comes to my shows, I ask her questions, she gives me advice.'

Later in the interview Gaga confessed that she found it difficult to identify with her contemporaries within the pop music industry, and was more inclined to mix with the older legends that she had admired her whole life because she found them to be more approachable. She explained that during the early days of her fame, she would be very guarded in her interviews and would hide behind her sunglasses and barely speak. However, when she met the likes of Elton John, she felt more comfortable and felt that she could be herself with him.

What irritated her, she added, was that some people still thought that Lady Gaga was merely an alter ego. But no: she maintained that Gaga and Stefani Germanotta were 'one and the same, there's no difference . . . I'm exactly who you say I am. I prefer Gaga because everyone calls me Gaga, even my mother.'

Her private life, she continued, was something she wanted to keep as private as possible, to the point where she was happy to lie about her personal relationships in an effort to protect the truth. She wanted to be seen as a performer, not a tabloid sensation. She didn't want her fans to be preoccupied with her weight or who she was seeing. However, with the constant scrutiny of the media, she admitted that most of the time she felt like she was onstage. 'I persistently believe that life is a stage and that life is *my* stage on which to be an artist. When I'm sleeping, it is an art: also when I am dancing, singing, making breakfast. However, there is a moment of freedom when, somehow, the stage disappears: when I cry. I would have to say most honestly when I cry, whether I'm onstage or offstage or alone or with someone, almost instantly when I cry, the stage disappears. Even when I cry onstage with my fans, somehow it becomes a living room and it's not a stage any more – there's something very honest.' (SHOWstudio.com interview)

Certainly, no one could accuse Gaga of not being honest in her interviews that summer. But while she had been pouring her heart out to the press she had also been busy putting finishing touches to the new material that would form her second album. In an interview with *Rolling Stone* in June 2010, Gaga excitedly gushed about the eagerly anticipated new record that she had been busy writing on the road. 'I've been working on it for months,' she told the magazine, 'and I feel strongly that it's finished right now. It came so quickly. Some artists take years; I don't. I write music every day.' Playing the reporter an excerpt from the song that we'd all eventually know as 'Born This Way', she enthused: 'That chorus came to me, like, I swear, I didn't even write it. I think God dropped it in my lap.' Of course, months later, when the track finally emerged and was likened by critics to Madonna's 'Express Yourself', it appeared to some that perhaps God had less of a hand in it after all. But more of that later.

During the interview with *Rolling Stone* she also put rumours to bed that she was suffering from a nervous breakdown. '[The media] have tried everything. When they start saying that you have an extra appendage, you have to assume that they are unable to destroy you. I've got scratch marks all over my arms and they say I am a heroin addict. It's from my costumes. When I pass out onstage they say that I am burning out when a) I have my own personal health issues and b) it's f***ing hot up there and I'm busting my ass every night.'

Gaga once again addressed the suggestion that she might be suffering from the condition lupus, though this time she was careful to squash speculation. 'I don't have it,' she assured the reporter. 'I'm a borderline lupetic person, which means I have it in my system and they don't know a lot about it. I don't want my fans to worry about it.' Asked if doctors had given her a regimen to follow to deal with the potential condition, she replied that as it was already in her family she didn't really listen to what the doctors said. Instead, she spoke to people who have lupus or her father, whose sister Joanne died from it.

But as Gaga had always maintained, she was a survivor, and she wasn't one to let a potential illness put her off her work. And for her, that part of her life was only going to get busier.

Chapter 25:
The Name's Jo

At the start of August, Lady Gaga returned to Lollapalooza – only this time, everybody knew who she was. The buzz surrounding the returning pop queen was immense and fans packed into the festival to catch a glimpse of the biggest star in the world. And she didn't disappoint.

Sporting once again a disco bra-and-panties combo similar to the one she had worn back in 2007, Gaga spoke confidently to the crowd. 'No one f★★★ing believed in me, but we did it. And look at all of us now.' Despite the fact that most attendees who had come to Lollapalooza were more into guitar rock than dance pop, the reaction from the crowd was on the whole positive, mainly because many first-timer Little Monsters had turned up to see their idol.

However, some critics weren't overly impressed with her antics. Amy Carr from *Time Out Chicago* said that from the beginning of the show, 'Gaga felt completely disconnected from her audience'. She added: 'Her opening number, "Dance In The Dark" took place almost entirely behind a curtain, with Gaga's silhouette vogueing every thirty seconds or so. At the end of the song, the diva simply panted into the microphone (a recurring theme) and stared, begging the crowd to . . . wait . . . for . . . it. When "it" finally came, it was a campy sketch in which one of her dancers fumbled with the engine of a broken-down car onstage, saying, "Oh noooooo! Now we'll never make it to the Monster Ball." "Yes you will," Gaga deadpanned, removing a purple mask that looked as if it came from a remake of *The Fly*. "I'll take you there." With such a ridiculous set-up, she had nowhere to go but up, but Gaga continued to play the diva card to a fault throughout the show, and the crowd abandoned her as a result.' The review went on to praise the spectacular set, however, adding: 'Her theatrics on the piano and an impressive run on a strap-on keyboard the size of a Christmas tree, combined with spot-on vocals, prove Gaga is no slouch.' But overall this particular critic couldn't get past Gaga's more surreal stage antics.

After her extravagant set, Gaga surprised Semi Precious Weapons fans by joining the band onstage during their performance, sending the crowd into a frenzy. Wearing little more than fishnet stockings and strategic golden pasties, Gaga rocked out on drums before stage-diving into the unsuspecting crowd. The revellers went wild as the singer skimmed over their heads. One fan got so excited he licked her stomach. 'If anyone calls Lady Gaga a pop star I'll f★★★king kill them,' lead singer Justin Tranter told the crowd over the roar of the music. 'She is a rock star, and she is helping Semi Precious Weapons bring rock 'n' roll back. Rock 'n' roll is back, b★★ches!'

Shortly after Lollapalooza, pictures were released of a rather dangerous-looking fellow by the name of Jo Calderone, who was to be the cover star of the September issue of Japanese *Vogue Hommes*. With his rugged looks, his greased quiff and serious pout, he looked like a James Dean throwback – as well as bearing an uncanny resemblance to a certain Ms Gaga. Pictures and video footage were leaked and it wasn't long before rumours started to fly that Calderone was actually Gaga's male alter ego.

Accompanying the set of pictures was an interview in which Jo revealed a little bit about himself. Apparently he hailed from Palermo in Sicily, he was a mechanic for his father's business and before the *Vogue* shoot he had never had his picture taken professionally. When he was asked how he knew Lady Gaga, he replied: 'I met her at a shoot Nick Knight was doing. She's f**kin' beautiful, and funny, and interesting. I was a little nervous for Nick to start shooting. She said, "Don't be, baby, you were 'born this way'." I took her out after.'

A year or so later, Gaga was asked by *V Magazine* about this Jo Calderone character and explained that he was 'created with [photographer] Nick Knight as a mischievous experiment'. She added in her typical Gaga way: 'After working together tirelessly and passionately for years, eating bovine hearts, throwing up on ourselves, Nick and I began to wonder: how much exactly can we get away with? How can we remodel the model? In a culture that attempts to quantify beauty with a visual paradigm and almost mathematical standard, how can we f*** with the malleable minds of onlookers and shift the world's perspective on what's beautiful? I asked myself this question. And the answer? Drag.'

It was then that they dreamt up the idea of a producing fashion editorial for *Vogue*, shooting the pictures in June 2010 under the working title 'Elegant Mechanics'. Shortly after the shoot, fashion site SHOWstudio.com released one 'live, straight-up and unretouched' picture a day showcasing this new model they had discovered. Fans and critics were divided by this strange experiment – but they were soon distracted by Gaga's next appearance, which was to make headlines the world over.

At the start of September, Gaga attended the MTV Video Music Awards. It was a great night for the star, as she scooped eight of the thirteen Moonmen for which she was nominated. Gaga arrived at the ceremony in a full-length Alexander McQueen dress with a Renaissance-style art print on the front, teamed with a gold-feathered headdress. This was the first of several outfit changes, each as elaborate as the last. But when it came to the award for Video of the Year, Gaga stunned the audience and viewers when she accepted it wrapped up in an artfully draped dress – made entirely of meat.

The dress, by Argentinian designer Franc Fernandez, was made of raw beef and was stitched on to Gaga backstage. As fashion statements went, this one was extreme even by Gaga's standards. Even rock legend Cher, who had handed her the award, was visibly stunned. However, to seasoned Gaga fans, the dress was simply the next step after the meat bikini she had worn on another cover for Japanese *Vogue Hommes*.

It could be art, it could be fashion, it might even be just an attention-grabbing stunt – but it had the world talking. Celebs at award ceremonies were renowned for pushing the envelope with outlandish gowns, but this was something else. PETA condemned the dress, saying: 'Wearing a dress made from cuts of dead cows is offensive enough to bring comment, but someone should whisper in her ear that more people are upset by butchery than are impressed by it.' The Vegetarian Society also released a statement that said that 'no matter how beautifully it is presented, flesh from a tortured animal is flesh from a tortured animal'.

However, feminist writer Laurie Penny said the dress presented Gaga as 'a woman in control of her own image and turning the tables on society'. She went on: 'It's a clever play on women being viewed as chunks of flesh, as pieces of meat, as things to be consumed. It's a sly wink at that aspect of society and the joke is on us. Just take her quip about asking Cher to hold her meat purse. She is the one laughing.'

The dress didn't just upset animal rights protesters, it also ruffled some feathers among members of the fashion and art worlds, who reckoned the dress was rather similar to Canadian sculptor Jana Sterbak's *Vanitas: Flesh Dress For An Albino Anorectic* from 1987. Regardless of the controversy, Gaga remained calm, remarking during an interview on the *Ellen DeGeneres Show* that the dress had many interpretations. 'For me,' she said, 'if we don't stand up for what we believe in and if we don't fight for our rights pretty soon, we're going to have as much rights as the meat on our own bones. And, I am not a piece of meat.' She also went on to explain that she was using the dress to highlight her distaste for the US military's attitude to homosexuals in the army with its 'don't ask, don't tell' policy that prevented openly gay people serving in the US forces.

This law, which meant gay people could serve within the army but faced expulsion if they revealed their sexuality, had left Gaga very angry. Although she knew President Obama was promising to repeal it, she was intent on making sure that happened, appearing at a rally in Portland, Maine, which particularly targeted the state's two Republican senators who were seen to be crucial in a Senate vote due several days later.

Eschewing her unusual and flamboyant dress sense, Gaga took to the podium wearing a conservative jacket and tie, and suggested a new policy should target the straight soldiers who were 'uncomfortable' with gay soldiers in their midst. 'Our new law is called "If you don't like it, go home!"' she said.

Speaking on behalf of gay soldiers, she said: 'Equality is the prime rib of America, but because I'm gay, I don't get to enjoy the greatest cut of meat my country has to offer. There are amazing heroes here today, whose stories are more powerful that any story I could tell, any fight I've ever fought, and any song that I could sell. I'm here because they inspire me. I'm here because I believe in them. I'm here because "don't ask, don't tell" is wrong . . . It's unjust, and fundamentally it is against all that we stand for as Americans.'

She went on to to criticize the Pentagon and senators such as John McCain, who had stated that homosexuals serving openly could cause disruption 'to unit cohesion and morale'. 'So what this means is,' she argued, 'that they're saying that straight soldiers feel uncomfortable around gay soldiers, and sometimes it causes tension, hostility and possible performance inadequacies for straight soldiers who are homophobic.'

She went on to suggest that under the current policy the wrong soldier was being penalized. 'Doesn't it seem to you that we should send home the prejudiced, the straight soldier who hates the gay soldier, the straight soldier whose performance in the military is affected because he is homophobic, the straight soldier who has prejudice in his heart?' she said. 'He gets the honour, but we gay soldiers, who harbour no hatred, no prejudice, no phobia – we're sent home?'

It was to be a year before President Barack Obama would officially repeal the rule that had barred soldiers from revealing their sexuality. Gaga was ecstatic about the news, taking to Twitter to say: 'What a tremendous & beautiful day, DADT is officially repealed & the new order is in place. Sending all my love & gratitude to service members.'

Meanwhile, as 2010 rolled to an end, Gaga received some good news. Earlier in the year, Rob Fusari had filed a $30.5 million lawsuit against the Grammy Award-winning performer, saying his protégé and former girlfriend had ditched him when her career took off. His argument was that he had introduced Lady Gaga to a record executive who helped her land a deal with Interscope Records, who had released *The Fame* and sold more than 3 million copies in the United States. Fusari acknowledged being paid around $611,000 but said it wasn't his full share, arguing that he had been denied a 20 per cent cut of song royalties, 15 per cent of merchandising revenue and other money owed.

In the lawsuit, Rob's lawyers revealed how he pushed Gaga to explore different musical genres, convincing her to give up on rock and focus on dance beats instead. He also argued that he was in part responsible for her choosing Gaga as her stage name.

Of more interest, the lawsuit also highlighted their closeness and how their working relationship swiftly became a romantic one, with Gaga sleeping over at Fusari's home and Rob hanging out with her family and dining at their Manhattan home.

Gaga had filed a countersuit, claiming the agreement she had with Fusari was 'unlawful'. But by the end of September both parties had agreed to drop their lawsuits and Gaga was able to carry on with her life. Meanwhile Fusari was himself slapped with a lawsuit from his old friend Wendy Starland, who claimed that Fusari had promised her that 'if she could find and introduce him to such a singer, they would work together to develop [her] and share equally in any revenues earned as a result.' (www.mtv.com) Starland says she agreed to those terms and introduced Gaga to Fusari, collaborating on songs and developing her musical and artistic style. At the time of writing the case remained unresolved.

Whatever the rights and wrongs of these lawsuits, Gaga didn't have time to dwell on them. She was too busy ensuring she was a relevant star who was mixing with the right people. In October, she joined Yoko Ono at the We Are Plastic Ono Band concert held at LA's Orpheum Theatre as part of a series of events honouring what would have been John Lennon's seventieth birthday. Despite the fact the gig was Yoko's tribute to her husband, Gaga grabbed the attention as usual in her skimpy crystal-studded outfit and super-high platform boots.

Gaga tweeted: 'WE ARE PLASTIC ONO. I got to sit in as a guest musician tonight, what a legendary band + mother, Yoko.' And if the excitement of performing with Yoko wasn't enough for her to deal with, then the news that her album had spent its 100th consecutive week on *Billboard* left her full of gratitude to her fans.

It wasn't all good news, though. Her Little Monsters were also there to support her when she discovered that her beloved grandfather Giuseppe was gravely ill. During one of her Monster Ball stop-offs in Nottingham, she dedicated her song 'Speechless' to him, telling the crowd: 'I don't always talk about my personal life but my grandpa's sick . . . So I was, like, crying all day, really sad. So I thought I might just be honest and tell you that's what's going on. So it's been one of those tough things that my grandpa's too old to come to my show, but I suppose if we sing loud enough, he'll be able to hear us. So this one's for you grandpa.'

Some days later, she, her family and ex-boyfriend Lüc Carl – whom she was rumoured to be seeing again – visited Giuseppe at his nursing home in New Jersey to say their goodbyes. The moment was a profound one for Gaga and would inspire one of her most popular songs, 'Edge Of Heaven'.

'When my grandma was saying goodbye [to my grandfather], there was something so intense that happened for me that I saw . . . as sad as the moment was, they both were acknowledging that they had really won in life because they had each other,' she told Howard Stern later, remembering her grandparents' sixty-year marriage.

She also told a story about how, a couple of days after the family had visited her grandfather, she and her father sat down at the piano at home and downed shots of tequila and chewed the fat. She said to her father, 'Grandpa's about to cross over into his glorious moment. It's hard now because he's on the edge.' As soon as the words had left her mouth, Gaga felt what would become 'Edge Of Heaven' flow out of her. She recorded it and played the tune to her grandfather over the phone. Hours later he had passed away. She explained that the song was 'about also knowing in your heart that you may never reach that glorious moment until you die, so live life on the edge – halfway between heaven and hell – and let's all dance in the middle in purgatory.'

Shortly after his death, she posted some lyrics on her Twitter site that would one day be the basis for one of her biggest hits: 'I'm on the edge of glory, and I'm counting on a moment of truth. I'm on the edge of glory, and I'm counting on a moment with you.'

Dozens of messages of sympathy and support for the star were posted by her fans and Gaga asked that in lieu of flowers, donations should be made to the Michael J Fox Foundation for Parkinson's research. It was a sad, personal ending to what had been a triumphant and headline-grabbing year.

PART THREE:
BORN THIS WAY

Chapter 26:

On the Right
Track, Baby

The past twelve months had seen Lady Gaga conquer the world. Her Monster Ball Tour had earned her a fortune, she had made headlines dressing as a man and wearing a meat dress, and she was winning more awards than she probably knew what to do with. Now her fans were desperate to hear the new material she had been working on while on the road. 'Born This Way' was the first new tune from what would be her second proper album, which would share the same title. Released globally on 11 February 2011, it topped the chart around the world, becoming only the twentieth song to debut at the top of the *Billboard* chart and the thousandth song to top it. As of January 2012, it also became the most downloaded song in iTunes history.

The song had been written in Manchester during her tour of the UK. Though she was keen to keep the new tune under wraps she had spent several weeks dropping hints, including singing a line from the song at the 2010 MTV Video Music Awards. In October that year, she tweeted lyrics from the chorus, to which

Perez Hilton replied with more lyrics. To whip the fans into a further frenzy, Elton John, who had heard the song, predicted it would become a new gay anthem.

Gaga explained to *Billboard* how the song came about: 'I want to write my this–is–who–the–f***–I–am anthem, but I don't want it to be hidden in poetic wizardry and metaphors. I want it to be an attack, an assault on the issue because I think, especially in today's music, everything gets kind of washy sometimes and the message gets hidden in the lyrical play.' Harking back to the early nineties, when Madonna, En Vogue, Whitney Houston and TLC were making empowering music for women and the gay community, she said: 'The lyrics and the melodies were very poignant and very gospel and very spiritual and I said, "That's the kind of record I need to make. That's the record that's going to shake up the industry." It's not about the track. It's not about the production. It's about the song.' She added in her *Transmission Gagavision* (a series of short internet broadcasts documenting her life) that 'Born This Way' showed she was 'an artist in a constant state of half–fantasy/half–reality at all times'.

The track proved to be a major hit across the world, and critics loved the high camp of the melody mixed with the positive message in the lyrics. However, there were some who were quick to dampen the excitement, suggesting that the song was too similar to Madonna's 1989 hit 'Express Yourself'. Among them, Neil McCormick of the *Daily Telegraph* claimed that the song was basically 'a reworking of Madonna's "Express Yourself" with a touch of "Vogue", which is a bit too much Madonna for someone who is trying to establish her own identity as the, er, new Madonna.' Despite Gaga saying the similarities between the songs was totally unintentional, even hardened Gaga fans could hear the striking resemblance, while some went as far as posting mash–ups of the two tunes on YouTube.

When she appeared on the *Tonight Show With Jay Leno*, she let slip that Madonna had sent her an email supporting 'Born This Way', adding,

'If the Queen says it shall be, then it shall be.' However, afterwards, Madonna's reps apparently said they were unaware that Madonna had been in touch with her.

Two months later, in an interview with *NME*, Gaga further defended herself. 'Why would I try to put out a song and think I'm getting one over everybody? That's retarded. I will look in your eyes and tell you that I'm not dumb enough or moronic enough to think that you are dumb enough or moronic enough not to see that I would have stolen a melody. If you put the songs next to each other, side by side, the only similarities are the chord progression. It's the same one that has been in disco music for the last fifty years. Just because I'm the first f***ing artist in twenty-five years to think of putting it on Top 40 radio, it doesn't mean I'm a plagiarist, it means I'm f***ing smart. Sorry.'

Yet in spite of the similarities, the song had seemingly hit the right spot with fans and Gaga was relieved that it was another massive hit. 'I can't believe it. I'm humbled, honoured and overwhelmed at the reception to "Born This Way",' she told *Billboard*. 'This has been so life-changing for me. Between *Billboard* and the international number 1s, and the radio numbers . . . I couldn't be more blessed to have the fans I have. I knew when I wrote the song it was special, but I also knew that perhaps my fans or my label were hoping for me to deliver "Bad Romance the Third" or "Poker Face the Third". I wanted to do exactly the opposite.'

If the song itself wasn't controversial enough, then the artwork was. In the black-and-white picture, shot by Nick Knight the previous December, Gaga is topless and showing off some tattoos on her back. Her make-up is heavy and strong and her hair is blown by the wind. What's more interesting is that there are rather sharp edges protruding from her temples, cheekbones and shoulders. Much was made of the strange body embellishments and for a while rumour had it that Gaga had undergone some kind of implant operation. However, it was later revealed that the strange alien look was achieved with prosthetics.

The video for the song had been in shot in late January in New York. Again directed by Nick Knight, it opened with Gaga giving birth before launching into a song that featured energetic dance routines, abstract images inspired by Salavador Dali and Francis Bacon, and a tattooed dancer called Rick Genest, otherwise known as Zombie Boy.

Choreographer and long-term Gaga collaborator Laurieann Gibson spoke to MTV and explained how the video came about. 'When she played [the song] for me, it took me a while to find out the visual interpretation that I could give back to her. And so I woke up one night and said, "I got it: We have to birth a new race." From the gate, Gaga was like, "I want Nick Knight for this video. I want a visual." She was always birthing something visual in her head, and Nick Knight is just, well, he's prolific but he's so genius. It was about pushing the bar of what a music video should be and can be. It's a different time; it's a different era; there are no limits. It is a viral message.'

Gibson went on to explain that it took some time for Gaga to master the choreography and the pair rehearsed at Alvin Ailey's Dance Theater in New York, where Gibson had studied dance years before. 'We rehearsed there because the choreography is really modern-based,' she explained. 'It's, like, more technical than anything she's ever done.'

The video was a big production, opening with Gaga declaring the birth of a new alien race that bore 'no prejudice, no judgement, but boundless freedom' before splitting into two opposing forces of good and evil.

The video, however, caused less fuss than her arrival at the 2011 Grammy Awards. Some may have wondered how Gaga could top the meat dress she had worn at her last awards ceremony – but she stole headlines yet again when she was carried down the red carpet encased in what looked like a giant egg. Her team told reporters that Gaga was in an embryonic stage and would be born onstage during her performance of the song.

Speaking later on *The Tonight Show With Jay Leno*, she claimed she was in the egg for three days. 'It was temperature controlled,' she said, adding: 'I was thinking about birth. I was thinking about embryos. Even my hair colour was a washed-out rose colour – it was meant to be a hair expression, an after-birth.' She went on to say that the performance was 'about birthing a new race, birthing a race within the race of already existing cultures of humanity – that bears no judgement'.

She also explained that the equally eye-catching performance at the awards – in which she and her dancers looked as though they were wearing outfits made from condom latex – had undergone some last-minute changes. 'Two days before the performances, I changed everything,' she said. 'I felt so bad because Haus of Gaga was red-eyed and up all night.'

Of course, Gaga not only performed at the show. She also went on to scoop three of six awards that she was nominated for – Best Vocal Pop album for *The Fame* and Best Short Form Video and Best Female Pop Vocal Performance for 'Bad Romance'. When asked how she celebrated her wins, she told Jay Leno: 'I don't remember very much. I know it was fun. I do remember being called Drunky Gaga at one point.'

Her 'condom' outfit at the Grammys may have turned a few heads, but it seemed a very deliberate choice of garment as she restarted her work with Viva Glam and continued her battle to get young people to practise safe sex. Since becoming the face of Viva Glam two years before, Gaga had helped raise $55 million for the MAC AIDS Fund via the sale of exclusive Viva Glam lipsticks. 'Safe sex has always been important to me, as for my generation, it's a most relevant consideration when you're growing up,' she told *USA Today*. 'I hope that young women know that sex is still a big deal, and they don't have to put out too soon. If they want someone to court them for a while before they give it up, that's wonderful and beautiful, and a man will only respect you more for honouring your body.'

She added that she hoped the campaign would not only raise awareness for AIDS and HIV but also to encourage people to love themselves and 'to honour your body and to use a condom or say no'. It was a message she was proud to share with her millions of fans worldwide.

Chapter 27:
More Controversy

In April, Gaga unleashed the second single from her *Born This Way* album. Like 'Born This Way', 'Judas' was a hi-NRG camp disco romp. Gaga explained that lyrically the song explored the negative parts of her life that she couldn't escape. She said on radio show *Last Call With Carson Daly* that the track was about falling in love with the wrong man over and over again, describing it as 'a very, very dark song'.

Speaking to MSN Canada, she expanded further: '"Judas" is a metaphor and an analogy about forgiveness and betrayal and things that haunt you in your life and how I believe that it's the darkness in your life that ultimately shines and illuminates the greater light that you have upon you. Someone once said to me, "If you have no shadows then you're not standing in the light." So the song is about washing the feet of both good and evil and understanding and forgiving the demons from your past in order to move into the greatness of your future.'

The video for the song was shot in mid-April, directed by Gaga and Laurieann Gibson, and saw Gaga in the role of Mary Magdalene and Norman Reedus as Judas. Needless to say, the religious overtones ruffled the feathers of the Bible brigade.

The video began with the disciples cruising down the highway on motorcycles, clad in scuffed leather jackets. Following behind is Jesus with Mary Magdalene and Judas behind them. Images of bar fights, a lipstick gun, and Gaga sharing a bath with Jesus and Judas occur throughout the video, which ends with Gaga being stoned to death by the crowd. 'I figured, if I'm going to get stoned for making this video, I'll stone myself first,' she told MTV, adding that the 'video really is just a metaphor' and not a 'biblical lesson'. She even laughed off the religious controversy, saying: 'In my opinion, the only controversial thing about this video is I'm wearing Christian Lacroix and Chanel in the same frame.'

Indeed, in an interview with *E!* presenter Giuliana Rancic, Gaga maintained the song was less about religion and more about ex-boyfriends like Lüc Carl, whom at this point she was seeing again. 'It's a metaphor for forgiveness and betrayal and darkness being one of the challenges in life as opposed to being a mistake.' She also told UK's MTV: 'I've had a lot of ex-boyfriends betray me – a★★holes, we all have them . . . I began to write a song about an ex-lover who betrayed me, who loved heavy metal music. And then I thought about the biblical implications and how Judas was the betrayer. And once I thought about what I wanted to do with the video . . . Judas didn't really betray Christ because he was part of the prophecy. So I thought a more liberating way to tackle the message of the song – we attack the idea by saying my ex betrayed me and this person haunts me, but I forgive them.' She added it 'was not meant to be an attack on religion'.

Co-director Laurieann Gibson echoed Gaga's words, telling the *Hollywood Reporter*: 'We don't touch on things that we have no right touching upon, but the inspiration and the soul and idea that out of your oppression, your darkness, your Judas, you can come into the marvellous light.' However, she did confess that due to her own religious beliefs, the video concept had been through several changes before the final version was chosen. 'At one point, there were two completely different views and I was like, "Listen, I don't want lightning to strike me! I believe in the Gospel and I'm not going there."'

And if anyone dared to disagree with the pair of them, Gaga had the final word. 'I don't think my fans are stupid. They're so smart, my fans, which is why I make the videos that I make because I know they understand the imagery.'

In May 2011 *Born This Way*, the album all her Little Monsters had been waiting for, was finally unleashed, shocking fans and critics alike with the cover image of Gaga as part-woman and part-motorcycle. The album, a mish-mash of techno, dance and rock, had a deeper lyrical content than before, and Gaga was exceptionally pleased with the record, commenting to *Vogue* that it was 'much more vocally up to par with what I've always been capable of. It's more electronic, but I have married a very theatrical vocal to it. It's like a giant musical opus theatre piece.'

In fact, and in spite of the critical and commercial success of her *Fame Monster* album, she reckoned that this new album was the 'absolute greatest work I've ever done'. Speaking to *RWD* magazine, she explained that the message, the melodies, the direction, the meaning, would offer her fans 'utter liberation'. 'I knew I had an ability to change the world when I started to receive letters from fans: "You saved my life." . . . "I'm gay and my parents threw me out." My fans have related to me as a human being and as a non-human being – as a super-human person that I truly am. Everyone tells me I'm arrogant but my music's the only thing I've got, so you'll have to let me be confident about one thing. I suppose that's what you can expect from the album: a lot of hit records that will p★★★ people off.'

One song she highlighted before the album's release was 'Yoü And I', which she described as a beautiful song that wasn't totally indicative of the new album sound. 'It's just a really big rock and roll hit,' she said. 'I do have these hopes that it could be a great crossover record, so I'm going to put my producer's hat on and get it to a place where I feel like it could reach the masses. It's a beautiful, beautiful lyric and melody.'

Fans across America dashed to snap the record up, buying an astonishing 1,108,000 copies in its first week. The album also debuted at the top spot in Australia, Austria, Brazil, Denmark, France, Germany, India, Japan, New Zealand, Norway, South Korea, Sweden, Switzerland, and Taiwan. In the UK, it sold 215,000 copies in its first week, more than the rest of the British top 10 albums combined.

One of the album's biggest fans was Gaga's friend Perez Hilton, who reckoned it was her *Like A Prayer*, which he said was 'huge praise coming from me, who is, like, the biggest Madonna fan ever'. He added: 'What's amazing about this body of work is that it really is that *Born This Way* is a body of work, where all of the songs make sense together. And it's as if she created this world or co-created this world with her fans, and all of these songs inhabit that world.'

Mexican producer Fernando Garibay, who worked with Gaga on *Born This Way*, admitted to the *Hollywood Reporter* that the recording of the album was something of a challenge. He explained that because Gaga was always touring or appearing on TV shows during its recording, they had to work hard to capture her moments of inspiration. 'We had laptops where we could go backstage and record something on the spot and we had a bigger set-up in the studio bus,' he recalled. 'When we needed to isolate vocals, we'd record in there, it felt more quiet. Then eventually when we actually made a stop somewhere for several days, we'd go into a real studio and flesh out these ideas.'

Garibay admitted that he wasn't just impressed by Gaga's work ethic, he was amazed by her voice. 'It's so powerful, you can pretty much capture it with anything, whether a laptop or a mic. It's funny, even vocals recorded off her laptop with the GarageBand mic we ended up using on the album. Sometimes we sacrifice quality for performance because there's a magic moment where the vocal sounds just right.'

As always, Gaga's team were very careful about the security surrounding the album. Although she had admitted before that she didn't mind people downloading her songs illegally, she wanted her fans to experience the songs when they were totally complete, and her people were forced to take extreme steps to ensure that none of the songs was leaked. Over the two or three months they were on the road, several attempts were made to hack into their email, so they decided to keep their computers offline all the time to ensure they were safe. Garibay reasoned that it was unfair for what he described as a 'sketch' to be released: 'To do it justice is to release a complete piece of art,' he told the *Hollywood Reporter*.

Many critics went wild for the album. The *NME* gushed, 'Gaga doesn't know when to hold back – and it's a damn good thing', honouring her for pushing musical boundaries to their 'ultimate degree'. *Slant* magazine said 'there was nothing small about this album, and Gaga sings the sh*t out of every single track', while Rob Sheffield of *Rolling Stone* praised her vocals and musical style, declaring that 'the more excessive Gaga gets, the more honest she sounds'.

But amidst all the plaudits, there were some cautious reviews. Randall Roberts of the *LA Times* reckoned Gaga lacked innovation, stating that 'musical adventure is not one of her strong points', adding: 'If Gaga had only spent as much time on pushing musical boundaries as she has social ones, *Born This Way* would have been a lot more successful.' The *Washington Post* described the album as 'boring' and suggested that 'at its worst, it sounds like reheated leftovers from some eighties movie soundtrack'.

Needless to say, Gaga's Little Monsters didn't listen to a word, and the album continued to break sales records across the globe.

Chapter 28:
Lüc Who's Back!

As Gaga had said time and again, her private life was private and in order to protect it, she maintained that she would be always outlandish as a pop star. The ploy worked. Over the years, there had been many more column inches written about her ridiculous garb than about her romantic life. While newspaper and magazine editors salivated over how to use the pictures, she was able to continue to lead a relatively private life. But since mid-2010, as her celebrity had reached a peak, it became inevitable that the press would want to know more about the woman behind the meat dress.

In June 2010, it was first reported that Gaga had reunited with her ex, Lüc Carl, after they were snapped together watching a Mets game at New York's Citi Field. They were also snapped kissing and cuddling in the St Regis Hotel swimming pool in Houston.

According to reports, the pair were reunited when Gaga walked into one of Lüc's clubs and started flirting with him, though unbeknownst to her he had another girl in the wings. 'Lüc was like the cat that got the cream,' a friend told the *Daily Mirror*. 'It could have ended really badly, but the other girl melted into the background. She knows what Lüc's like – he has women all over

194

the place . . . Gaga has convinced herself that this time she's got Lüc back for good.' After that meet-up she invited him along to watch the Mets game and they were inseparable from that moment on.

By October, the press was having a field day about the couple's relationship, claiming they had 'married' in a 'spiritual commitment ceremony'. Gaga and Lüc had apparently declared their love in an 'intimate moonlit service' in Crete. 'They both dressed up and said beautiful handwritten vows,' a source told Glamourmag.com. 'They then exchanged rings in a spiritual service and drank shots before sitting down to a lovely private dinner at a tiny restaurant. They wanted to show that they are committed to each other and want to spend the rest of their lives together. They are still planning to marry, but that will come later when she has the time to plan a big Italian-style wedding.'

However, in May 2011, during an appearance on *The Graham Norton Show*, Gaga said that she didn't have a boyfriend, and that she hadn't been on any dates. And in yet another interview she said the pair remained very good friends. What was the truth? Well, she was not the type to spill the beans.

Coincidentally, the next single to be released from the album was the sensational ballad she had raved about earlier in the year, a song that she claimed was inspired by her troubled relationship with Lüc. She told *Rolling Stone* that without him, she might not be where she was today. 'I wouldn't have been as successful without him,' she said. 'I've never really loved anyone like I loved him. Or like I love him. That relationship really shaped me. It made me into a fighter. After I broke up with him, I promised myself I would never love again and would make him rue the day he doubted me. But then I again moved back to him. [It was] love. But, you know, I don't really know much about love . . . I suppose if I knew everything about love, I wouldn't be good at making music, would I? I wrote this new song "Yoü And I", it talks about us, me and him.'

Ironically, however, it would be the video for this song about Lüc that would finally close the door on this part of her troubled love life and open up another romantic avenue for Gaga.

On the set of the video, Gaga met hunky Taylor Kinney, a jobbing actor who had appeared in such shows as *The Vampire Diaries*, *Bones* and *Shameless*. In the video he played the ripped love interest and spent much of the clip in a bath with Gaga dressed up as a mermaid. Although Taylor would later admit he fell for her shortly after they met, it was some months later that the couple went public with their relationship, and almost a year before either would speak about being together. At the end of 2012, after the couple had reportedly split and reunited, Taylor revealed that he had fallen for Gaga because she shared his mother Pam's outlook on life. 'I look up to a strong woman, maybe that's why I fell for Gaga,' he told *Extra*. 'She works incredibly hard and is very strong and inspirational like my mom, with a great work ethic.' He also said he was keen to start a family at some point, claiming: 'I think I'd be a good dad; it would be a pleasure. I'd love it and I'm in my thirties now. My mom wants me to get married, and have children of course. She's met Gaga, we've been dating a while, we're in a committed relationship and I'm really happy.' However, he did admit that the biggest obstacle in their lives was the time they spent apart. Luckily, with his regular role on the TV show *Chicago Fire*, he had the means to keep up with her. 'I use all the money I make on flights to see the people I love. If I spent it on fancy cars, homes and material stuff I wouldn't be able to do that. I have the freedom to see the people I care about – my girlfriend and my family. Gaga and I rely on space ships, very fast transport, to see each other.'

With *Born This Way* smashing up the charts it came as no surprise that Lady Gaga continued to be nominated for endless awards. And at the VMAs in August 2011, she once again took the audience by surprise. There was no blood, no meat dresses, no eggs – instead this time she took to the stage as Jo Calderone, her alter ego, who had recently appeared on the cover artwork of 'You And I' and had featured in a cameo role in the video.

Wearing a loose black suit and T-shirt with her black hair greased back off her face, Gaga – as Jo – staggered out on to the stage, puffing on a cigarette, and told the audience about his tortured relationship with the pop star. 'Lady Gaga, she left me,' he raged. 'She said it always starts out good . . . She said I'm just like the last one.' The performance left some of the celebrities such as Katie Holmes and Katy Perry open-mouthed, as they tried to get their head around this performance art. After Jo's monologue, he sat at the piano and burst into a rendition of 'Yoü And I'. Halfway through the song, he jumped up on the stage and performed a dance routine with a bunch of similarly dressed male dancers, before Queen legend Brian May stepped onstage for a guitar solo.

Speaking after her performance, Gaga said she thought it would be an interesting cultural exercise to create someone who wasn't her. She told *Vanity Fair*: '[He is] someone infinitely more relatable than me. A blue-collar Italian guy in a Brooks Brothers suit who just wants this girl to stay the hell home. It took a performance piece for me to understand things about who I am. And through doing this [with acting coach Larry Arancio] I learned about how I am in bed. I said, "Isn't it strange that I feel less able to be private in private and more able to be private in public?" And Larry said: "Well, maybe that's the problem." And I said that's exactly the problem – when I am onstage I'm so giving and so open about myself. And when the spotlight goes off I don't know what to do with myself.' She went on to explain that Larry had told her that in preparation she should write everything down. One of the things she wrote was that whenever she had an orgasm, she would cover her face, a fact that she used in her performance when Jo said: 'When she comes, she covers her face like she doesn't want to see, like she can't stand to have an honest moment when nobody's watching.'

After her MTV performance, Gaga surprised her fans again by taking a new musical direction. In October, Tony Bennett released a second album of musical duets, teaming up with Gaga on the track 'The Lady Is A Tramp'. The pair had worked together earlier in the summer and Tony said in an interview with *Rolling Stone* that he was impressed by her talent and work ethic. 'She came in so prepared and so knowledgeable about what to do. She's as good as Ella Fitzgerald or anybody you want to come up with,' he said. 'And that's without her dancing and her philosophies about breaking myths that are incorrect and social situations. She's very strong. I know it sounds way out, but she could become America's Picasso if they leave her alone and let her just do what she has to do. She is very, very talented.'

The pair performed the track on TV as the opening number on Gaga's ABC Thanksgiving special, *A Very Gaga Thanksgiving*. The show also featured several stripped-down, acoustic versions of songs from her second studio album along with two Christmas songs. TV anchor Katie Couric interviewed Gaga about her life and the inspiration behind her music, and in another segment she met up with third-graders from her old convent school.

Gaga was proud of the show, as she knew her father would like it. 'I actually directed it. It's the first of two things I directed,' she said. 'I directed this as well as the video for "Marry The Night", my new single . . . So we'll be watching that and eating turkey and doing what all New Yorkers do, which is getting ready for every window to be filled with Christmas cheer the next day.'

Around the time of the show's screening, she released the track 'Marry The Night', an eighties-sounding rock/popfest with echoes of Giorgio Moroder. The video told the story of when she was dumped by Def Jam. In an interview with *E!* she explained that certain scenes in the video were autobiographical, particularly those set in a clinic.

'Although it is autobiographical, there is an element of surrealism. It recounts a day in my life when I was in the hospital, but on that same exact day I was dropped from my record label. If you give up after that you are never destined to be an entertainer.' She added: 'It was important to me to push the boundaries to show the reality of how terrifying it was. And how I can twist what happened into something victorious.'

In the opening scene she is seen bruised and obviously drugged-up, being wheeled through a clinic on a gurney by two nurses who are wearing next-season Calvin Klein. 'The first seven minutes are the insight into my creative process. It's my internal monologue, not just as I felt then, but as I do now.'

The concept of the video may have been rather highbrow but the straightforward pop song was a hit with her fans and critics, though it was one of her lowest-charting singles worldwide, perhaps because so many people already owned it via the album. However, her performances were more eccentric than ever. When she performed the track on *The X Factor* in the UK, she stunned viewers by appearing onstage dressed as a decapitated corpse in a flowing black gown. The macabre performance also included an enormous black crucifix, a confessional box, quasi-mystical torches and, of course, hunky dancers. At the start of the spin-off *Xtra Factor*, after patchy contestant Kitty Brucknell had been voted off, a more normal-looking Gaga dashed across the stage and hugged the distraught young wannabe. When presenter Caroline Flack tried to interview Gaga, she ignored her and dragged Kitty off for a drink.

It was reported around the same time that after years of collaboration, Gaga and Laurieann Gibson had parted company after a spat. However, it wasn't until March 2012 that Laurieanne would finally reveal the real reason why they cut ties. 'No judgement,' she told *Entertainment Tonight*. 'But it just got a little dark for me, creatively. I think it just reached the point where I wanted to keep the brand that I had helped build a little purer and still accessing the kids, and it was fun for me. But it gets difficult when it gets a little dark and heavy.'

As 2011 came to a close, Gaga was able to look back at another triumphant year in which she had achieved so much and broken many boundaries. She had released another critically acclaimed album, completed 202 shows in 28 countries with her Monster Ball Tour, generated global headlines and given so much back. When she took part at the Robin Hood Foundation benefit in New York City earlier in May, she was one of the very few artists who refused to accept the usual six-figure fee, instead insisting that the money go to the anti-poverty programmes in the city. She also teamed up with her mother Cynthia to launch the Born This Way Foundation, which was set up to foster a more accepting society, 'where differences are embraced and individuality is celebrated'. The Foundation, it states on its website, is dedicated to creating a safe community that helps connect young people with the skills and opportunities they need to build a kinder, braver world.

Later in the year, Gaga channelled Marilyn Monroe when she serenaded former US President Bill Clinton at a concert honouring the tenth anniversary of his foundation and his sixty-fifth birthday. After she crooned 'Happy Birthday', she said, 'Bill, I'm having my first real Marilyn Monroe moment. I always wanted to have one. And I was hoping that it didn't involve an accident with some pills and a strand of pearls, so here we are.'

In addition to the release of her records, she also published a book of candid photographs taken by her friend Terry Richardson, entitled *Lady Gaga X Terry Richardson*.

As early as September 2010, Gaga had spoken about working with the photographer. 'Terry wanted to do a book about the Monster Ball. He wanted to shoot me backstage, not onstage, and look at who I am offstage,' she revealed in *Vanity Fair*. 'He's on the bus with me. He just follows me everywhere. He'll photograph me when I'm changing – those quick changes during the show. And sometimes I'll have to pee during the show, and I'm always screaming, "Terry, get out!" And he'll be saying, "It's so beautiful. You're so punk!"

If only my fans knew I was peeing in a beer cup backstage.'

In the foreword to the book, Gaga gushed even more: 'Sometimes it seems as though I've waited my entire life to be photographed by Terry Richardson. With Terry, the relationship extends beyond the photograph, and if you're really lucky he will teach you something truly profound about yourself. I have discovered through him that "shame" is an obsolete notion and "apology" is an injustice to any performance. Perhaps it is his kind eyes behind those famous glasses, or the giggling noise he makes at 4:00 in the morning when he's caught me in bed. Click, giggle, click, click, click, beautiful.'

Yet despite the fact she had achieved so much, Gaga still had so much to conquer in 2012, once she'd performed in Times Square on New Year's Eve. In fact, nothing was going to stop her.

Chapter 29:
Madonna Expresses Herself Again

For the January 2012 issue of *Vanity Fair*, Lady Gaga took writer Lisa Robinson back to her home on the Upper East Side, the first journalist to be allowed within the walls of her family home. As she prepared pasta and tomato sauce in the kitchen, Chanel-clad Gaga explained how her mother had been her style inspiration. 'I was very much like my mother. She would do her hair every morning and get dressed nice. So most of the time I would stay up all night straightening my hair and I would even put my make-up on before bed sometimes so that when I woke up in the morning it would be ready for school. I just had to be glamorous. It made me feel like a star.'

Later, Cynthia showed Lisa around the basement, which was still strewn with Gaga's possessions. It became apparent that the singer wasn't ready to commit to a place of her own. She even denied the rumours from the previous year about her planning to set up home with Lüc Carl. 'Gypsy queen couldn't take the leap,' she said. 'I can't commit to being an adult – I'm not ready.'

Later in the article, Gaga took Lisa downtown to show her where she got her education. Joined by her schoolfriend Bo O'Connor, she recounted the times they'd hang out in bars and wait to buy drugs and how she'd woken up one day on her tour bus and decided never to take drugs again.

In the interview, she went on to confirm that she was dating someone new but wouldn't elaborate any further as to whether or not the lucky man was Taylor Kinney. 'I can't imagine that people sit and talk for hours about their marriages and relationships,' she said. 'It seems strange to me . . . The only thing I am not always forthright about is my relationships because I think it's not classy to exploit your relationships.' However, Gaga did confide that she had 'never felt truly cherished by a lover', stating: 'I have an inability to know what happiness feels like with a man. I have this effect on people where it starts out good . . . and then they hate me.'

She reasoned that men often descended into a 'whose–dick–is–bigger?' contest with her, explaining that if she was able to write a song quickly, they'd end up getting upset at how effortless it was for her. 'It's a hideous place to be in when someone that you love has convinced you that you will never be good enough for anyone. I had a man say to me, "You will die alone in a house bigger than you know, with all your money and hit records, and you will die alone."'

Meanwhile, as Gaga was exposing her thoughts within the pages of *Vanity Fair*, her idol Madonna was being less supportive. Possibly peeved that Gaga had pretty much overshadowed her during the past couple of years, the Material Girl said in an interview with ABC that her influence on Gaga's music was 'interesting' and 'amusing'. 'I certainly think she references me a lot in her work,' she said drily. 'And sometimes I think it's amusing and flattering and well done. There's a lot of ways to look at it. I can't really be annoyed by it.' And when asked what she had thought about the similarities between 'Born This Way' and 'Express Yourself', Madonna coolly replied: 'When I heard it on the radio, I said that sounds very familiar.' Asked if that felt annoying, Madonna responded, 'It felt reductive.' This gentle ribbing of Gaga continued when in another interview, with *Newsweek*, Madonna described 'Born This Way' as 'a wonderful way to redo my song. I mean, I recognized the chord changes. I thought it was . . . interesting.'

Later in the year Madonna and Gaga would go head to head again when, on her poorly received MDNA Tour, Madonna cheekily included a 'Born This Way'/'Express Yourself' mash-up. Gaga, never one to get involved in a public battle, remained quiet on the matter, although she did say during a performance in New Zealand that: 'It sometimes makes people feel better about themselves to put other people down or make fun of them or maybe make a mockery of their work, and that doesn't make me feel good at all. That just makes me feel like I'm not being a good human being.' At least Gaga could be comforted by the fact that 'Born This Way' had topped the charts in nineteen countries and had become the fastest-selling song in iTunes history. However, by the end of 2012, relations between the stars remained chilly. During a show in Minnesota, Madonna told the crowd: 'I have the best fans in the whole world. So take that, Lady Gaga! You know, I invited her onstage to sing with me. But, she turned me down. It's OK. I've been rejected before. It builds a little character.'

In February, Gaga's dad Joe opened a restaurant at 70 West 68th Street called Joanne Trattoria, which he had been renovating for the past few months. 'This has been a lifelong dream, and I couldn't be happier that it's finally happening,' he told New York's *Daily News*. The chef, Art Smith, added: 'This is truly a collaborative effort, inspired by the Germanottas' love of food and family. Everything from the menu to the decor has a bit of their family in it. It's why everything is so warm and approachable.'

The restaurant was described by the *New York Times* as having a 'well-stocked bar', a cosy fireplace and seating for about seventy people. The walls were covered with scenes of the Tuscan countryside, and Germanotta family photos hung near the entrance. The restaurant had been a labour of love for Joe and he was thrilled when it finally opened its doors. However, reviews left a little to be desired.

The *New York Post's* Steve Cuozzo wrote that the calamari he was served was 'like leather' and the 'shellfish pasta [was] similar to airplane food'. He claimed that some of the food was 'the worst I've had in a lifetime'. In his article, entitled 'You'll Gag on the Food at Gaga's', Cuozzo did not take any prisoners. 'You don't expect a brand-new eatery to be running on all cylinders,' he wrote. 'But Joanne, owned by the pop superstar's parents, last night was running mainly on acrid-smelling burnt vinegar wafting intermittently through the raucous dining room.'

But by July of that year, the restaurant seemed to be doing well, and Joe and Cynthia had found their feet. In a video interview with the Men Who Dine blog, Joe said: 'The first night, it was crazy because everybody was camped out here. And I kept saying to people, "She [Gaga] is not going to come to opening night. She's a little busy getting ready for the tour."'

Later in the year, Joanne's would receive even more press when critics sniped that during Gaga's sold-out Born This Way Ball, which had kicked off its 110 dates in Seoul in April, she had put on considerable weight.

At her Amsterdam gig, during which she also caused controversy by smoking a joint, Lady Gaga sported a fuller than usual figure. But despite the interest from the media Gaga merely shrugged off the criticisms and happily admitted that she had gained around twenty-five pounds. She claimed she didn't care what people thought and said it was her father's tasty restaurant tucker that was partly responsible.

'I love eating pasta and pizza,' she told Elvis Duran on his radio show. 'I'm a New York Italian girl. That's why I have been staying out of New York. My father opened a restaurant . . . It's so freaking delicious, but I'm telling you I gain five pounds every time I go in there. So my dad wants me to eat at the restaurant, and I'm, like, I've got to go where I can drink green juice' (to cap it all, in August NYC's health department gave Joanne's a C grade for numerous violations).

However, despite the fact she said she wasn't too worried about her weight gain, she did intend to lose some of the timber. In a rather contradictory statement, she said on Elvis Duran's show, 'I'm dieting right now, because I gained, like, twenty-five pounds. And you know I really don't feel bad about it, not even for a second. I have to be on such a strict diet constantly. It's hard because it's a quite vigorous show, so I tend to bulk up, get muscular, and I really don't like that. So I'm trying to find a new balance.'

Coincidentally, all of this focus on her body size led to Gaga launching a 'body revolution', posting unedited pictures of herself in underwear on Twitter. For the first time she admitted that as a youngster she had endured eating disorders as she struggled to fit in and deal with her own body image. 'My weight/loss/gain since I was child has tormented me,' she wrote in a blog. 'No amount of help has ever healed my pain. But you have,' she said of her Little Monsters. 'When I eat and am healthy and not so worried about my looks, I'm happy.' She added: 'My boyfriend prefers me curvier. This is who I am. And I am proud at any size. And I love you, and want you to be proud in any form you may take as well.'

Her strong words achieved what she hoped as she received responses from her fans. 'I have been startled and overwhelmed with pride and emotion these past few days.' she wrote. 'Watching you all create a safe space online for people to be compassionate is the greatest gift you could ever give me.'

In an interview with *Stylist* in the UK, Gaga said she aspired to be as confident as global superstar Adele. 'I thought, well, I don't really care if they think I'm fat, because, quite honestly, I did gain about thirty pounds. Adele is bigger than me, how come nobody says anything about it? She's so wonderful and I think her confidence is something I have to match. She has set the bar very high for a lot of women.'

She also admitted that she thought the way the press had dealt with her weight gain was laughable. 'I was acutely aware of some photos on the internet – my mom called me and was like, "Did you gain weight?" – everybody was telling me about it, and I didn't really care. But when I heard it was on the news, where they talk about wars, the economy crashing and the election – I just thought, "This is f★★★ing ridiculous." I mean, what kind of example is that to a young girl sitting at home?'

Meanwhile, Gaga was continuing to tour the world with her Born This Way Ball. Although the critics and fans were mostly blown away by the impressive staging of the show – which she described as 'an Electro-Metal Pop-Opera; the tale of the Beginning, the genesis of the Kingdom of Fame. How we were birthed and how we will die celebrating' – it did come in for a fair bit of criticism, in particular in Asia, where several religious groups viewed the tour as Satanic. This resulted in various protests, including one from the Islamic Defenders Front, who brought about the cancellation of a show in Jakarta where Gaga was denied a licence to perform.

During her time on the road, Gaga as usual continued to work on songs for her next album, to be titled *ARTPOP*. One of the potential songs was a track she performed during the Twickenham leg of the Born This Way Ball. Entitled 'Princess Die', she told the crowd the track was her way of showing her appreciation for the late Princess of Wales, who died in 1997 in a car crash in Paris. 'Since I was a very young girl, the People's Princess was the most important person in me and my mother's life,' she said, adding, 'I swore if I ever had an audience like this in London I would take a moment to appreciate her. This song is called Princess Di – D-i-e . . . I predict controversy, but I don't care . . . Let's take a moment to appreciate her presence and what she means.'

Gaga also dedicated the track to the singer Amy Winehouse, who had died in 2011 aged twenty-seven. The death of the young star, whom Gaga had once been mistaken for at Lollapalooza, had hit her hard. 'It really affected me quite deeply,' she told *Rolling Stone*. 'She was my only hope when I was up and coming. Nobody knew who I was and I had no fans, no record label and everybody, when they met me, said I wasn't pretty enough or that my voice was too low or strange. They had nowhere to put me. And then I saw her in *Rolling Stone* and I saw her live. I just remember thinking "Well, they found somewhere to put Amy . . . " She's really special. She just gave me a lot of hope and she deserved a lot better than what people gave her.'

The best accolade was to follow when, at the close of 2012 at a fundraising event, Amy's dad Mitch suggested that Gaga would be the perfect person to play Amy in a planned biopic – and that Brit tough man Ray Winstone could play him.

Aside from the newie 'Princess Die', another song called 'Cake', tipped to feature on the next album, appeared online, sending fans into an inevitable frenzy. The rappy song, which sounded like nothing Gaga had previously released, was accompanied by a video that saw a naked Gaga in a hot tub being spanked by another woman In other respects, too, the song was a little more grown-up, with its aggressive, profanity-laden lyrics. When the video appeared online with a reference to Terry Richardson, fans were unsure whether or not the song was an album track or soundtrack or title of a new book collaboration with the famed photographer. As usual, Gaga liked to keep her fans guessing.

Chapter 30:
The Scent of Things to Come...

Singers may release records or star in films or write books, but if they don't have a scent as well then they're pretty much lagging behind. So at the start of 2012, Gaga confirmed ongoing rumours that she too would be unleashing a scent on the unsuspecting world later in the year.

Of course, as it was Gaga, fans expected that it would be far from a traditional one. In fact, Gaga made it clear that this fragrance would be like no other, mentioning in an interview on *The Kyle and Jackie O Show* in Australia as far back as 2011 that the scent would smell 'like an expensive hooker' and that it would feature fragrance notes of 'blood and semen'.

When the perfume – named 'Fame' – was eventually launched in September 2012, Gaga laughed off these earlier comments. 'I was just pulling everybody's tail,' she giggled, during an interview with TheKit.ca. 'I would just do that all the time. Because until you define what a celebrity fragrance means, does it matter what it smells like? I mean nobody really cares, do they? You buy the fragrance because you like the artist, right?' She went on to explain that she wanted to create a perfume that actually smelt good and that people would want to buy, regardless of whose name was on the bottle.

In place of blood and semen, the perfume's ingredients included tears of belladonna, crushed heart of tiger orchidea with a black veil of incense, pulverized apricot and the essences of saffron and honey drops. 'What I like about it for me is I love the smell of apricot,' she told *Good Morning America*. 'And I love the belladonna smell because it has a dangerous sort of muskiness to it. It's a plant that can kill you but also smells quite delicious. And I also really love the honey drops. These are all just things that I really like to eat also. They're things that I would eat during sex as well as wear, if that makes any sense.'

If we hadn't quite got the message, she added that she would wear the scent when she wanted to seduce someone. 'I wanted it to be a very slutty perfume,' she said, claiming that she wanted a fragrance 'that was desirable, and which is quite nice for not only just, you know, a young girl like me, but for any woman that wants to go home to their husband and lay down and feel like a queen.'

What made the perfume unique was that it would be the first ever black eau de parfum – the liquid was black but would turn clear when it was sprayed. This clever marketing ploy was just one of the ways by which Gaga wanted to make her perfume stand out in the overcrowded market. 'I have always felt disappointed by celebrity fragrances because they seem to ride on the air of amateur or cheap, like the fans don't deserve the same as someone buying a fragrance at Chanel deserves . . . You shouldn't wear [my fragrance] if you're not likely to look for a lover, because it's going to attract them.'

Fame's advertising campaign, shot by Steven Klein, also helped to make an impression, featuring as it did a totally naked Gaga with tiny men crawling over her body. The result? The celebrity-endorsed perfume enjoyed the most successful launch in history, selling more bottles in one week than any other celebrity fragrance of 2012.

Gaga continued on her world tour, stopping off in South Africa and South America. She also found time to do a spot of shopping – albeit done by a minion – and snapped up several items belonging to Michael Jackson, including his infamous white glove. Gaga told her Twitter followers that 'the fifty-five pieces I collected today will be archived and expertly cared for in the spirit & love of Michael Jackson, his bravery, & fans worldwide.'

Gaga ended her year still campaigning her heart out, in particular with regard to gay marriage. In September Pope Benedict XVI told French bishops that 'Marriage and the family are institutions that must be promoted and defended from every possible misrepresentation of their true nature, since whatever is injurious to them is injurious to society itself.' Gaga hit back on the French radio station Europe 1, saying: 'I think that gay marriage is going to happen. It must. We are not actually equal – humanity – if we are not allowed to freely love one another. What the Pope thinks of being gay does not matter to the world. It matters to the people who like the Pope and follow the Pope. It is not a reflection of all religious people.'

At the start of December she expressed her 'gratitude' to Russian Prime Minister Dmitry Medvedev for opposing regional laws that made it a crime to provide young people with information about homosexuality. Three Russian cities had recently passed bills imposing fines of up to $150,000 (£95,000) for providing minors with information on homosexuality, which the laws term 'homosexual propaganda'. However, when asked about the laws, Medvedev said in a televised interview that 'not all relations between people can be regulated by law'.

Meanwhile, the Born This Way Ball continued to rattle on as it crossed the US and Canada. Fans turned out in their thousands to see their icon do her thing, and do it brilliantly. But what can fans expect once *ARTPOP* has hit the shelves? Can Gaga continue to innovate, and surprise and challenge us?

The past year would suggest that she has chosen to slow things down. The avant-garde fashions of old seemed to take a back seat and for a time Gaga opted for a sophisticated – dare we say normal? – look, such as the Versace dress – which Liz Hurley famously wore at the *Four Weddings and A Funeral* premiere – which she slipped on to meet Donatella Versace in Italy. And then there were the pics of her in South America in denim shorts and a bra top – a casual look that she swore she'd never let her fans see. Could her relaxed attitude be something to do with her relationship with Taylor Kinney, which seems to be going from strength to strength (or at least was at the time of writing)? Or is this 'normal Gaga' yet another example of performance art? Who knows?

All we know is that Gaga is a one-off, a star unlike any other to have emerged on the scene over the past decade. And only three albums in, she still shows she has promise and the ability to surprise, to shock and to satisfy all at once.

Sources

NEWSPAPERS AND MAGAZINES

Age, The
Billboard
Blackbook
Blender
Daily Mirror
Daily Star
Daily Telegraph
Elle
Entertainment Weekly
Fabulous (*News of the World* magazine)
Guardian
Heat
HX
i-D
Independent
iProng
LA Times
Maxim
Music News
New York magazine
News of the World
Observer

OK!
Rolling Stone
RWD
Seattle Weekly
Sun
Sunday Times Culture
Telegraph (South Australia)
Vanity Fair
Women's Wear Daily

ONLINE

About.com
AllMusic.com
Blogcritics.org
EarSucker.com
GayWired.com
Guitarcenter.com
Hitquarters.com
Kidzworld.com
MTV.com
PopEater.com
Shockhound.com
SHOWstudio.com
SongwriterUniverse.com
SoundOnSound.com
Superstarmagazine.com
TheBackBuilding.tumblr.com
WomenswearDaily.com
Wustl.edu (The Washington University of St Louis)

TV

Lady Gaga interview with Jean Paul Gaultier,
  CW TV, September 2011
Lady Gaga: Inside the Outside, MTV, May 2011

The Brit Awards, 2009, 2010, ITV
The Graham Norton Show, BBC1, May 2011
The Jonathan Ross Show, ITV, October 2011
The Paul O'Grady Show, Channel 4, June 2011

BOOKS

Callahan, Maureen, *Poker Face: The Rise and Rise of Lady Gaga*,
  Hyperion, 2010
Phoenix, Helia, *Lady Gaga: Just Dance – The Biography*,
  Orion, 2010
Richardson, Terry and Lady Gaga, *Lady Gaga X Terry Richardson*,
  Hodder & Stoughton, 2011

PHOTO CREDITS

Page 1: Splash News (*top left and right*); Paul Morigi/WireImage/Getty Images (*bottom*)

Page 2: Daniel Boczarski/Redferns/Getty Images (*top*); Veronica Ibarra/FilmMagic/ Getty Images (*bottom*)

Page 3: Michael Loccisano/FilmMagic/Getty Images (*top left*); Charles Eshelman/ FilmMagic/Getty Images (*top right*); Dave Hogan/Getty Images (*bottom*)

Page 4: Noel Vasquez/Getty Images

Page 5: Brian J. Ritchie/Rex Features (*top left*); WENN.com (*top right*); Tabatha Fireman/Redferns/Getty Images (*bottom*)

Page 6: Mark Campbell/Rex Features (*top left*); KPA/Zuma/Rex Features (*top right*); Gregg DeGuire/FilmMagic/Getty Images (*bottom*)

Page 7: Erik Pendzich/Rex Features (*top*); Sipa Press/Fex Features (*bottom*)

Page 8: Dimitrios Kambouris/WireImage for Marc Jacobs/Getty Images

Page 9: Lester Cohen/WireImage/Getty Images (*top left*); Startraks Photo/Rex Features (*top right*); Leon Neal/WPA Pool/Getty Images (*bottom*)

Page 10: Dave M. Benett/Getty Images (*top*); Brian J. Ritchie/Hotsauce/Rex Features (*bottom*)

Page 11: Kevin Kane/WireImage/Getty Images (*top*); Rex Features (*bottom left*); Erika Goldring/FilmMagic/Getty Images (*bottom right*)

Page 12: Matt Sayles/AP/Press Association Images (*top left*); Sipa Press/Rex Features (*top right*); Kevin Winter/Getty Images (*bottom*)

Page 13: David Wolff-Patrick/Getty Images (*top*); Brian Rasic/Rex Features (*bottom*)

Page 14: Ray Tamarra/Getty Images (*top left*); Wong Maye-E/AP/Press Association Images (*top right*); Jeff Kravitz/FilmMagic/Getty Images (*bottom*)

Page 15: Steve Granitz/WireImage/Getty Images (*top left*); Rob Kim/Getty Images (*top right*); Evan Agostini/AP/Press Association Images (*bottom*)

Page 16: Gareth Cattermole/Getty Images

The author and publishers are grateful to the following for help with this book: Louise Dixon, Judith Palmer, Katie Duce, Ana Bježančević, Lindsay Davies, Glen Saville, Adrian Laing and Andrew John.

INDEX